471/-

The Myth of the Mahatma

By the same author

A History of India
Asia in the European Age
British India 1772–1947
The Last Years of British India
Nehru: A Political Biography

Michael Edwardes

THE MYTH
OF THE MAHATMA

Gandhi, the British and the Raj

UBSPD
UBS Publishers' Distributors Ltd.
5 Ansari Road, New Delhi-110002
Branches:
New Delhi ● Bombay ● Bangalore
Madras ● Calcutta ● Patna ● Kanpur
Offices Abroad: London ● Chicago

Constable · London

First published in Great Britain 1986
by Constable and Company Limited
10 Orange Street London WC2H 7EG
Copyright © 1986 by Michael Edwardes
Set in Linotron Ehrhardt 11pt by
Rowland Phototypesetting Limited
Bury St Edmunds, Suffolk
Printed in Great Britain by
St Edmundsbury Press
Bury St Edmunds, Suffolk

British Library CIP data
Edwardes, Michael, *1923*–
The myth of the Mahatma
1. Gandhi, M. K.   2. Statesmen – India
– Biography
I. Title
954.03′5′0924   DS481.G3

ISBN 0 09 466070 0

Heaven smiles and faiths and empires gleam
Like wrecks of a dissolving dream

Hellas P. B. Shelley

CONTENTS

ILLUSTRATIONS

PREFACE

Why yet another book about Mahatma Gandhi and the British Indian Empire, especially by someone who has already written fairly extensively about both? Recently there has been considerable media exposure of both the Mahatma and the Empire he is widely supposed to have brought to its knees, thereby securing his country's independence. First came the hagiolatrous and historically misleading movie, produced by Richard Attenborough with the financial assistance of the Indian government. After its screening in 1982 and the subsequent raft of 'Oscar' awards, Attenborough's *Gandhi* acquired the status of a fountain of truth, in spite of widespread criticism of its simplistic images and 'epic' distortions of reality.

Then came *The Jewel in the Crown*, a TV reworking of the novels of Paul Scott, a hugely enjoyable, dramatic entertainment which soon acquired a very similar truth-rating to that of the *Gandhi* movie. *Jewel* conjured up an exotic vision of a dying empire, at once brutal and bizarre, its ruling class consisting mainly of bullies and psychotics, as if the Raj actually had been a drama (a sort of *Marat-Sade?*) played out in a lunatic asylum in which even the staff was not entirely normal.

As if this were not enough, *Jewel* was followed by a screen adaptation of E. M. Forster's *A Passage to India*, perhaps the most influential of the many bad novels written about the Raj.

Not unexpectedly, such popular and easily digested historical pap produced a fall-out of revisionist debate in the Press, with articles by expatriate Indian novelists and others which clearly demonstrated their authors' love of myth rather than reality.

Of course, there is little new in this. On a somewhat more discreet level, ever since the assassination of M. K. Gandhi in 1948, the Mahatma industry—a sort of fan-club of mainly Western academics, journalists, churchmen, minority demagogues and pop radicals, with the benevolent support of successive Indian governments—has perpetuated and enhanced certain myths, in the main those with contemporary political implication, concerning the life and significance of its hero. Naturally, the epic story of one man's struggle against a mighty empire takes on the mythic qualities of the conflict between Darkness and Light, Good and Evil. Myths of such appealing simplicity have been the stuff of romantic literature in both East and West for thousands of years. The trivialization of great men and great events in the interests of an hour or two of entertainment does no great harm. But when mythic activity becomes a sort of philosophical springboard for militant activism in the real world, then ignorance of the facts behind the myths becomes a positive menace—and not only to those who so casually accept them.

It is that menace—fortunately still more potential than actual—that is the excuse for what follows, which is not intended as either a biography of Gandhi or a history of the Raj, but a series of interlinked commentaries upon the factual, rather than the mythic, nature of British rule in India and that of its most publicized opponent.

Eastbourne, March 1985

DEATH IN DELHI

15 August 1947

The precise moment of death was surprisingly dignified, in an appropriately Eurasian manner: to the sound of conch shells and the striking of an English clock. The chimes at midnight marked the end of Britain's Indian Empire, the glorious Raj, that brightest jewel in the British Crown, as Benjamin Disraeli had so eloquently, and not all that inaccurately, called it. When the then Tory prime minister coined his metaphor, some seventy years before, the Raj had appeared powerful and vigorous, and remained outwardly so until the outbreak of World War II. But the cancer was already in the bloodstream, sapping the vitality and undermining that sense of purpose which had first established the Empire and then preserved it.

Missing from those who waited in the Constituent Assembly building for the midnight hour was a conspicuous figure —Mahatma Gandhi, the one who, according to widespread belief, had done most to hurry along the death of the Raj. The Mahatma saw little cause for celebration: an India divided into two new nations; a spreading violence between the Hindu and Muslim communities. Nearly a thousand miles away from Delhi and its tarnished imperial splendours, living in a decaying mansion in a Calcutta slum, the Mahatma was trying to reduce the religious terror—and succeeding, though the scale of the tragedy was too large even for him. Thirty-two years of struggle had, he said, come to 'an inglorious end'.

[13]

30 January 1948

The Raj had been dead for just over five months, but the carnage that had surrounded the birth of its successors continued, claiming more than half a million lives. At least twelve million people had been forced to leave their homes in what was probably the greatest cross-migration in history— Muslims to Pakistan, Hindus and Sikhs to India. No wonder the Mahatma had answered those who wished him well on his seventy-eighth birthday in October of the old year, 'Where do congratulations come in? Would it not be more appropriate to send condolences. . . ?'

The new year had brought no surcease. With a fast, the Mahatma could create an interregnum, but no more. Indeed, after the momentary quiet, the noise of violence renewed, seemed even louder. The last fast had been in Delhi, where the Mahatma lodged in the anything but decaying mansion of a multi-millionaire industrialist. It was in the garden of this house that he held his regular evening prayer meeting.

On the next to last day of January, with a pleasant coolness in the air, some 500 people gathered to see and hear, to touch the feet, or catch the eye, of the Mahatma. It was a little after five in the afternoon when he emerged from the house, his hands resting on the shoulders of two female disciples. As he approached, the crowd broke to surround him. Their greeting was answered by the Mahatma with the traditional Hindu gesture of bringing his hands together, like a kneeling saint in a stained-glass window.

Turning towards the wooden platform on which he would sit, the Mahatma came face to face with a stocky man wearing a blue sweater, who, without greeting, fired three shots from a small hand gun. Hit in the chest and abdomen, the Mahatma fell to the ground. In a few moments he was dead.

The next morning, as the body of the apostle of non-violence passed us, borne to the cremation ground on a gun carriage surrounded by troops, an Indian friend remarked that *now* the Raj was really dead. At the time, I dismissed the judgement as absurd, the product of highly emotional circumstances, but I soon recognized that my friend had a profounder understanding of the relationship between the Mahatma and the Raj than I had.

The occasion was, in a way, a moment of truth, for to an already existing, though rather academic, fascination with India's religion and culture was added an almost overwhelming desire to know more than the schoolbook superficialities about the history of the Raj I had watched dying, and of those who had made it, ruled it, fought it, profited from it, often suffered and not infrequently died because of it.

Part One

MAKING
THE RAJ

I

COMPANY OF MERCHANTS

In the fourth decade of the nineteenth century, Count Magnus Bjornstjerna, a shrewd Swedish statesman, and then his country's ambassador in London, asked himself a question—and then went on to give at least part of the answer.

> But who, then, is the conqueror, who the sovereign of this immense empire over which the sun extends so gloriously his glittering rays, that has arisen on the continent of Asia as if by enchantment, and now rivals in extent that of Alexander, Tamerlane or Nadir Shah?
>
> Why, on an island in another quarter of the globe, in a narrow street, where the rays of the sun are seldom able to penetrate the thick smoke, a company of peaceable merchants meet; these are the conquerors of India; these are the absolute sovereigns of this splendid empire.

The 'company of peaceable merchants' had first been given a charter to trade between the Cape of Good Hope and the Straits of Magellan by Queen Elizabeth I of England in the last year of the sixteenth century. There had been no idea of territorial dominion then, but only dreams of profit—in spices, silks, gems, camphor and indigo, in the luxuries of the Gorgeous East. In fact, the first target was not India at all, but the Spice Islands of the Indonesian archipelago. In 1608, however, the Company's agents in Bantam and the Moluccas reported that the people there were good customers for Indian calicoes, and suggested that a trading post should be set up in India to buy them.

At that time, most of India was ruled by the Mughals, a Muslim dynasty founded in 1526 by a direct descendant of Tamerlane and Jinghiz Khan. His great-grandson, the fourth emperor, Jehangir, gave permission for such a post to be established, and finally—in face of strong opposition from the Portuguese, who had been the first Europeans to arrive in the East—the Company established warehouses at Surat, the chief port in western India, in 1612. After Surat, further 'factories' (as the trading posts were called) were set up at Ahmedabad, Burhanpur, Ajmer and Agra.

By 1622 the Company had nothing more to fear from the Portuguese, who had suffered a series of defeats at the hands of the English and the Dutch. But the English themselves had been soundly defeated by the Dutch in the Spice Islands between 1618 and 1620, in spite of the fact that England and Holland were nominally allies in Europe. When, in 1623, the Dutch in Amboyna seized ten Englishmen and nine Japanese, tortured them into confessing to a conspiracy to assassinate the Dutch governor, and executed them, the Company turned its face away from the East Indies and towards India.

By 1647, the Company operated twenty-three Indian establishments, but the civil war between king and parliament in England almost proved disastrous. The Company's pepper cargoes were seized by the king and guns meant for the Company's ships were requisitioned by parliament. For a while, the abandonment of Eastern trade was considered. Even when, in 1655, arbitration produced £85,000 from the Dutch in reparation for the Company's losses at Amboyna in 1623, the Company saw less than half the sum. Cromwell, in urgent need of money, borrowed £46,000 of it 'for twelve months' and never repaid it.

With the restoration of Charles II, better times came. The Company received a new charter, and the right to coin money and exercise jurisdiction over English subjects in the East. In 1668, in exchange for a substantial loan, the king transferred Bombay—part of the dowry his wife, Catherine of Braganza, had brought to him six years earlier—to the Company.

Within the Mughal Empire, there was anarchy and unrest, mainly due to the Islamizing and anti-Hindu policies of the sixth Mughal emperor, Aurangzeb. Hindu merchants began to look for some place of safety. They suggested that, if they were offered adequate protection, they would move to Bombay with their families and, presumably, their businesses. This was a tempting proposition, for the Dutch were trying to take over the Portuguese stations on the Malabar coast of India, the French (whose own company had been formed in 1668) were beginning to establish factories on the same coast, and commercial competition showed signs of becoming intense. Furthermore, the power of the warlike Marathas, a loose confederacy of Hindu rulers, was increasing and they had already, in 1664, attacked Surat. In 1669, therefore, the chief merchant of Surat began to fortify Bombay as the new headquarters of the Company's interests in India. It was the beginning of a new phase for the East India Company. The 'quiet trade' so dear to the directors in London was to be defended by the Company's servants in India, and in that defence lay the origins of the British Empire.

In 1674 the Maratha, Sivaji, enthroned himself as an independent king, and an Englishman, Henry Oxinden, was officially present at the coronation. He returned with a peace treaty which he believed would prove of 'no small benefit' to the Company's affairs. Sivaji had realized that British naval expertise might make the Company a valuable ally in his wars against the Mughals, particularly since a Mughal fleet—sheltering near Bombay during the monsoon—occupied its energies by raiding the Maratha coast. Unfortunately, the combined depredations of Sivaji and the Mughal admiral had an almost ruinous effect on the trade of Bombay. Even Sivaji's death in 1680 brought no relief. His son attacked the Portuguese and plotted to take Bombay. Pirates infested the coast and the interior was in continuing disorder.

Bombay had grown fast, its military strength and religious tolerance making it a haven, not only for Hindus escaping the Mughal terror, but for Christians fleeing from the Inquisition in Portuguese Goa. When it was taken over by the English, Bombay had had a population of 10,000; by 1674 it was a city of 60,000 inhabitants. But the Company's employees were badly paid and subjected to salary cuts and petty economies at the slightest excuse. When Aurangzeb, for example, reimposed a poll tax on non-Muslims, the Company protested, whereupon the emperor increased customs dues from 2 per cent to 3½ per cent. The resultant miserliness on the Company's part brought protests from the garrison, never happy under its merchant bosses, and further discrimination against the armed forces led to rebellion. The garrison commander, one Richard Keigwin, in 1683 assumed authority in Bombay in the name of the king. He tightened up the city's defences and, when the Mughal admiral arrived in 1684 for his usual wintering in the harbour, he was ordered to leave—and went. Ultimately, in exchange for a complete pardon, Keigwin surrendered to a fleet sent from England.

On the other side of India, in Bengal, the Company's agent, Job Charnock, blithely declared war on the entire Mughal Empire in 1686 over a quarrel about customs dues. The Company's ten ships and 600 men—all that were available in the area—proved inadequate for the task, and the English were forced to abandon their conquests and their factories and flee to Madras. In the end, a treaty was signed, and in 1690 the Company's ships were moored once again in the Hugli river, near a spot where Charnock founded what was to become the capital of British India. In 1696, the English were given leave to fortify Calcutta, and a fort—named in 1699 Fort William, in honour of the Dutch king of England—was erected. In the same year, the three villages of Chutanuti, Govindpur and

Calcutta were rented from the Nawab of Bengal. The Company had become an Indian landowner.

The Company's possessions, as distinct from agencies or trading stations, were now four in number—Fort St George, Madras; Bombay; Calcutta; and, acquired at almost the same time as Calcutta, Fort St David opposite the town of Cuddalore on the Coromandel coast. The Marathas, who had acquired the last town in the course of their free-booting activities, sold the site and all the land within 'ye randome shott of a piece of ordnance'—a method of property dealing which so appealed to the English that they sent to Madras for the gun with the longest range and the most expert gunner! This demarcation by artillery was carried out in September 1690, and the villages within the radius are known to this day as 'cannonball villages'. Of the Company's four possessions, Madras was by far the most efficient and vigorous; Elihu Yale, whose name is perpetuated in Yale University, was governor from 1687 to 1692 and applied anti-piracy laws with great severity against Indians and English alike.

Matters were not running smoothly for the Company in England. Sir Josiah Child, who saw it as the Company's duty to lay the foundations of British dominion in India, had purchased for £80,000 from Charles II a prohibition against British subjects competing with the Company in India. But in 1694, the English parliament passed a resolution against the Company's monopoly and expressed the opinion that all English subjects had an equal right to trade in the East Indies. In 1697, Spitalfields silk-weavers demonstrated against cheap imports of Indian textiles. In 1698, Child's commercial rivals—offering the government a loan of £2,000,000 at 8 per cent—were granted a charter for a rival company, and the New English Company was founded. It fared badly, however, having first lent almost all its capital to the Crown, and then employed men who had been dismissed by the old Company.

In 1702, the two companies agreed to an armistice, and six years later they amalgamated.

In 1707, the last great Mughal Emperor, Aurangzeb, died. The anarchy that followed was to give both Britain and France the opportunity—and the incentive—for empire. Just as they began to feel their strength, the great central land power began to fall apart and an enveloping chaos threatened.

2

ARMY OF MERCENARIES

'Let us strike at the trunk of the withering tree and the branches will fall by themselves.' With these words (uttered by a Hindu leader in 1723) northern and central India entered a period of disruption which was to last for nearly a century and out of which the British were to emerge as the supreme power in the country.

In the crumbling world of eighteenth-century India, what was happening in Europe became the catalyst of significant events there. Wars between Britain and France in the West became wars between their trading companies in India. With conflict came visions of a wider dominion than the paltry confines of a trading post. To fight their wars—against each other and against the Indian rulers who became their allies and puppets—each acquired an army of mercenaries, Indian soldiers trained in the European manner and officered by Europeans. With these men, and with those no less effective weapons, corruption and intrigue, the English East India Company acquired Bengal after 1757, becoming in 1765, by a grant from the then fugitive Mughal emperor, an *Indian* ruler and legally a feudatory of the Empire.

From Bengal came immense profits, but again not for the Company. By 1772 its directors were forced to confess that only an immediate loan of £1 million from the British government could stave off bankruptcy. From that moment they were no longer the 'absolute sovereigns' of a growing empire, for though they got their loan, they also had to take 'an Act for establishing certain regulations for the better management of the affairs of the East India Company, as well in India as in

Europe'. This Act opened the door to more coherent interference in the administration of the Company's Indian territories.
Through it, in 1784, came legislation which, though it left to
the directors of the Company the lucrative and influential gift
of patronage, placed the Company under the direct supervision of the British government. A board of control was
established with a president at its head. The board could
overrule the directors, and the head of the Company's administration in India could not be appointed without its approval.

It was a system which invited and intensified conflict. The
directors of the East India Company were suspicious of the
government and of its agent, the governor-general. They
feared, and rightly so, that the politicians in London would
want to expand British dominion while they themselves simply
wished to maintain trade, expanding only if the profit was sure
and the expense minimal. Their hope of dividends rather than
dominion was as doomed as the dinosaur.

As the eighteenth century came to a close, two powers in
India seemed poised upon the edge of empire, that invisible
line which when crossed leads to both dominion and defeat.
The *mise-en-scène* of these times of decision was anarchy, a
great anarchy filling the vacuum left by the collapse of another
empire—that of the Mughals which, under the blows of
foreign invaders and domestic ambitions, had contracted into
the shadows. But the Mughal emperor, though he inhabited
those shadows and was a shadow himself, still exercised a
peculiar fascination over the minds of the men who were
destroying his empire. They yearned for legitimacy, in the
same way as the destroyers of Rome had yearned for it, as the
ironmasters and manufacturers of nineteenth-century Europe
were to yearn for it—desirous of hiding their unromantic
origins and mundane activities behind titles which were the
highest award of an aristocratic social order. In India, the
Mughal emperor occupied a position of almost mystical importance, derived from a glorious past. From the titles he could

bestow, titles rich with romantic resonances—Defender of the Realm, Sword of the State—the *parvenus* gained the sanction of history for the realities of their position. The desire for a place defined by tradition was particularly compelling in India, for society there was, and to a large extent still is today, carefully stratified. In the case of the Hindus, the vast majority of India's people, caste controlled not only social but political relationships. In the case of Muslims, the Mughal emperor and his satraps appeared as another and superior caste. The two emerging contenders for the Mughal Empire desired status *in Indian terms*. For one of them, it was not unnatural; they were Indians themselves. For the other, it demonstrated only a sensible pragmatism. The first were Marathas. The second, the British.

As the British established themselves on the coastline and then began their slow and not particularly sure movement inwards into India, they and their European rivals reduced the number of powerful elements who, as Mughal authority collapsed, had claimed independence. In 1784, Warren Hastings, who laid the foundations of British dominion in the face of much opposition, wrote: 'It seems to have been the fixed policy of our nation to enfeeble every power in connexion with it.' What he meant was that power allied with purpose and ambition had attracted dependants and sycophants. Once powerful rulers on the periphery of the two main power groups had recognized that, their security lay in moving delicately in the orbit of one or the other of them. In politics, as in astronomy, large bodies exert a gravitational pull.

It took until 1819 for the British to settle with the Marathas and with the consequences of that settlement. Then, as one of those responsible put it: 'The task of conquest was slight, in comparison with that which awaits us, the preservation of the empire acquired.'

Certainly none of the men who had been responsible for the acquisition of that empire doubted the magnitude of their achievement or of what now lay before them. The Company was unquestionably the supreme power in India, and the country was theirs to do with what they liked. Not that the future lacked its dangers. Another of the conquerors feared that 'universal conquest' might create more disturbances. Yet another was sure that the introduction of British law and administration to the newly conquered territories would 'excite agitation and alarm'. But if they had some doubts about the future, it was a distant future. The immediate problem was the settlement of central India, although this did not stop them from thinking about what was to come or what had been. They were not overwhelmed by their achievements, but all were rather surprised at the completeness of the victory.

In retrospect, they had every reason for surprise. In less than eighty years a body of merchants from a small country thousands of miles away had managed to gain control of a vast empire; and one not filled with savages, but containing an ancient and highly sophisticated civilization of its own. Some of the men who had built this empire were very conscious of the fact. The civilization they saw was in decay but still in many ways vigorous and colourful. They responded to it without arrogance. They did not suggest that they were the purveyors of a higher civilization but they did believe that it was their duty to bring order out of chaos, to establish peace and security in place of anarchy, cruelty and violence. It was not an unworthy motive for conquest, even though the British had themselves contributed to the chaos.

There were also coarser, less responsible motives. The expansion of British power had been supported by influential politicians in London, not because they were dreamers of empire, but because they saw the potential profits of conquest. The men on the spot in India may not have had much personal concern for trade, but their masters in London—and, particularly, successive British governments—were anxious to create a suitable climate for business, an empire based upon commerce, although not the commerce of the East India Company. The Company was certainly sovereign, but by no means absolute. And the real conquerors were the traders and the mill-owners who had broken the Company's trade monopoly in 1813.

Whether without these incentives, without the engine of ambition and optimism propelled by a rapidly industrializing Britain, the Company would have been forced to expand anyway, is another matter. There is an interior logic to territorial expansion. It is always necessary to occupy a little more territory than is actually wanted in order to defend the piece already held. The British were subject to this logic the moment they ceased to be ordinary traders and, in the middle of the eighteenth century, took up arms. Once they had been drawn into the vortices of Indian politics, at a time when the central authority of the Mughal Empire had collapsed, inactivity on the Company's part would have meant its replacement by another European power. Such a situation was unacceptable in terms both of trade and of political rivalries in Europe.

The why of Britain's conquest is reasonably clear. *How* the British were able to conquer so much of India, so many differing principalities and powers, is not quite so simple. It had nothing to do with the alleged superiority of Englishmen over Indians, the racial explanation of imperialism so dear to nineteenth-century theorists of empire. There were certainly remarkable men, but leadership of a high order was not displayed by all the British, nor was it a British monopoly. The difference lay in the competitive nature of individual Indian leadership and the communal, or national, quality of the British. Indian leaders were concerned with creating their own position and sustaining it against the ambitions of others, usually their own supporters, adventurers like themselves. The British had no desire to overthrow the government of their fellow-countrymen. In part, it was the contrast between ambition uncontrolled and ambition disciplined, a contrast of purposes,

[29]

which gave the British their supreme feeling of confidence. They knew that, in times of crisis, they could rely on the support of their fellows, with whom they shared a similar outlook.

The ability to conquer did not rest on the fact that the British had more military expertise than their opponents. Some of the European-trained armies of Indian princes were quite as good as the Company's forces, just as well armed, and not infrequently better generalled. But these armies were usually led by soldiers of fortune whose main aim was to satisfy their own ambitions, even if it meant changing sides or using their own strength to set up as independent rulers. The British, when they fought, were out to win—and not just one battle but a whole campaign. For them, a defeat was merely a temporary affair. Its effect could be cancelled in the next engagement. It was this sense that no single defeat could be final which gave victory to small British forces against what seemed to be incredible odds. Once a number of such victories had been won, the British became convinced that even the most powerful of enemies could be defeated.

Another factor on the British side was that they could not only concentrate resources upon some given area but replenish them once they were exhausted. This was a matter both of economics and of maritime mobility. The British could move reinforcements, human and material, by sea from Britain or round the coasts of India. If things went badly in one place, they could compensate from another. Not so the Indian rulers. They had nothing to draw upon, for their defeat was someone else's gain. Furthermore, the revenues of Indian princes were continually decreasing, and not simply because of anarchy. The Indian economy, in general, was contracting, while the British in the first flood of the Industrial Revolution possessed a rapidly expanding commerce.

The British, then, had the means relatively well organized

and continually expanding. They had, too, their sense of solidarity, the belief that their actions not only satisfied personal ambition and the commercial interests of their employers, but were also to the general, if often undefined, advantage of the British nation.

India had little to counteract this. The artificial but functional unity of the Mughal Empire, which had maintained peace and, generally speaking, encouraged production and trade in the interests of the central government, had been destroyed. Its successors collected their revenue by plundering. Nor was there any sense of nationalism where community was divided from community by caste, and men of one religion from those of another by the most impenetrable of walls, that of tradition and custom. The only example of anything that might have been called nationalism in the European sense was that of the Marathas in the seventeenth century. Their unity had its origins in a shared hatred for Islam and the Mughal rulers who represented the political face of that religion. But by the middle of the eighteenth century Maratha nationalism had faded. With the threat of Mughal power removed, the Maratha leaders contended for power amongst themselves while extending their personal control over parts of the carcass of the Mughal Empire.

This lack of nationalism made it possible for the British to conquer the country by swallowing it piecemeal. It also made their conquest acceptable. Power was the criterion of empire, and Indian rulers who knew so intimately the realities of power themselves felt no shame at accepting the rule of those who were capable of exercising it. The essence of that power was the military might of the forces of the East India Company.

These forces had steadily grown in size as the conquest of India progressed. By 1857, the Indian element had reached the then enormous number of 233,000 men. Though the Company had some all-European regiments (about 15,000 men) as well as units hired from the British Crown, white troops were outnumbered by nearly seven to one.

In 1857, a mutiny by Indian troops of the Company's army was to shake British rule in India to its foundations.

Rioting in Bombay 1948

Gandhi, assassinated by a Hindu extremist on January 30th 1948, is cremated on a sandalwood pyre on the banks of the Jumna river.

Fort St George, Madras, painted by George Lambert and Samuel Scott

Fort William, Calcutta, painted by George Lambert and Samuel Scott,
c 1731

Warren Hastings (1732–1818), Governor-General of India. Portrait by
Sir Joshua Reynolds

Suttee. Engraving by B. Picat

Lord Canning, the first Viceroy, decorates Indian princes at a Durbar at
Delhi after the mutiny of 1857.

Charles Cornwallis, first Marquis, by Arthur Devis, c 1795

3

TRIBE OF GUARDIANS

On the surface, the rebellion of 1857 may appear as a conflict of religious beliefs, a battle between rival gods. In fact, it was a bloody and violent clash between the old and the new in India, between tradition and modernity, nostalgia for the past and fear for the future—the scenario, in effect, of what today is known as the 'development process'.

The rebellion originated in the reaction of a conservative, tradition-loving section of Indian society to the zeal of their British conquerors. As the British consolidated their power in India, they also seemed to be intent on reforming Indian society both morally and politically. In creating a rational and efficient administration, they threatened much of the traditional order. Princes and landowners, the principal representatives of that order, felt themselves under sentence of extinction.

Under the governor-generalship of Lord Dalhousie (1848–56), both the princes and landowners had felt the heavy hand of government. Dalhousie wished to remove as many feudal states as he could, leaving only a few of the larger ones nominally independent, but actually under the control of the central government. The plan was laudable in many senses, for it was designed to lead to better government and a happier situation for the peasantry who, under their feudal princes, had no rights or protection against the whims of the ruler. Dalhousie first used his powers to annex states where there was no direct heir, refusing to accept the custom that a childless ruler had the right to adopt an heir. Satara, Jhansi, Nagpur and a number of minor states were annexed. The kingdom of

Oudh, which had been grossly misgoverned for many years, was also made a part of British India.

Dalhousie's second objective was to expropriate land from landowners without 'proper' title to their estates. Some 20,000 were confiscated in the Deccan alone.

Because the government was a foreign government, and its agents foreign, too, often with only a slight understanding of customary law and even of local languages, there were many cases of injustice which the government did little to remedy. The reforms were carried out ruthlessly, with little or no attempt to consider the feelings of those involved. It is small wonder that those who suffered were angry, or that those who expected to find themselves in the same position were frightened.

Indians only had to look around them to see the British interfering at every level of life. In the twenties and thirties of the nineteenth century, a number of reforms had been carried out. Suttee had been banned, infanticide suppressed, and a campaign mounted against the Thug gangs who robbed and murdered in the name of the Hindu goddess Kali. These warts on Hindu society had been regarded with horror by the British, who had also allowed themselves to view the Hindu religion as a barbaric, pagan creed, beneath contempt. Many officers in the Company's army took this attitude, and grasped every opportunity of trying to persuade their men to become Christian.

Some of the sepoys, as the Indian soldiers were known, felt that an attempt would be made to break their caste in such a way as to cut them off from their religion. Hinduism, unlike Christianity, is indivisibly part of the social order. Man's place in society is carefully ordered by the mechanism of caste. Break a man's caste, and not only is his place in society destroyed but he stands on the threshold of a damnation far worse than the Christian concept of hell. A Hindu believes that reincarnation continues until the highest caste—the Brahmin—is reached

[34]

after the soul has returned many times and has suffered much. When a Brahmin dies, his reward is oblivion, the heaven of the Hindus. Many of the sepoys in the Company's army were Brahmins and therefore felt that they had everything to lose from the Christianizing activities of the British. There had, in fact, been mutinies based on similar fears before 1857.

In Vellore in south India, the sepoys had revolted in 1806 after being ordered to wear a new style of headdress, to trim their beards, and to give up wearing caste marks. This, they believed, was an attempt to make them Christians. The mutiny was brutally suppressed. In 1824, a sepoy regiment which had been ordered to Burma refused to move, because it felt its caste was endangered by an official refusal to supply special transport for cooking pots; caste usage compelled each man to have his own set. Guns opened fire on the sepoys on the parade ground where they were assembled, and next morning six of the ringleaders were hanged, while hundreds were condemned to fourteen years' hard labour on the public roads. Five more men were later executed and their bodies hung in chains as an example to their fellows. In 1852, another regiment refused to cross the sea to Burma. This time, however, the sepoys were simply marched away to another station. A number of other mutinies and near-mutinies had taken place, all with some basis of fear that the British were trying to break the sepoys' caste and make them turn Christian.

By the end of 1856, the whole of India—and particularly the north—was uneasy. Nearly every class had been shaken in some way by reforms and political changes instituted by the British. Only the most Westernized Indians were unaffected by fear. The newly emerging middle class had no wish to preserve the old order unchanged, and during the rebellion they remained actively loyal to the British. But the dispossessed had been awaiting their opportunity. Those princes who had lost the territories they felt to be rightly theirs, the king of Oudh, the last sad descendants of the Mughal emperors at the twilight court of Delhi—all were awaiting the opportunity to rise in rebellion. Their agents were active among the sepoys, playing upon their fears and exciting their apprehensions, recalling the tale that a hundred years after the Battle of Plassey would come the day that saw the end of British rule. The fuel was ready for the fire; all that was needed was a spark. The British themselves provided it.

In 1857 it was decided to replace the old musket known as Brown Bess with the new Enfield rifle, which had a much longer range and infinitely greater accuracy. To load the new rifle entailed biting a greased cartridge. The sepoys believed, with some justification, that the grease was made from cow or pig fat—the first from an animal sacred to the Hindus, and the second from an animal regarded as unclean by the Muslims. The Hindu sepoys saw this as yet another attempt to break their caste as a preliminary to making them all Christians. Slowly at first, but with increasing momentum, sepoy regiments refused to accept the new cartridges and finally broke into open mutiny. To them rallied the disaffected. At last the opportunity had come to make a stand against the British and, with the Bengal army at their backs, the disaffected seemed to have every chance of success.

Essentially, the Mutiny which had been triggered by dissatisfaction in the Bengal army was a feudal reaction to the pressures of British dominion which had been felt at all levels of the community. Behind the rebels there temporarily coalesced a wide and conflicting range of interests. There has been much controversy—engendered in the main by Indian historians—about the 'national' character of the Mutiny. There was none. Among the feudal elements involved, there was merely a desire to return to things as they had been before the coming of the British. The sepoys rebelled in what they believed was self-defence. Not unnaturally, other elements took advantage of the breakdown of law and order. In some areas, there were distinctly Luddite overtones when mobs

[36]

attacked and destroyed factories and machinery. This may well have been partly a product of class antagonisms, for there was a general tendency to attack those who had benefited from British rule—bankers, money-lenders and the like, who were also merchants and entrepreneurs.

One of the principal factors in the suppression of the rebellion was the fact that most of the leading rebels were united only on one simple issue, the ejection of the British. When this seemed impossible to achieve, everything else fell to pieces. The sepoys fought on—not for any ideal, but because the British had made it quite clear to them that the chances of death if they surrendered were about as high as, if not higher than, they would be if they went on fighting. Most of the civilian leaders either disappeared, or were killed in battle or executed. The men who had taken impromptu advantage of the effective collapse of British rule faded into the background from which they had emerged.

The bloody events of 1857–9 represent a divide in the history of British India. The rebellion was, in general terms, the violent meeting of two dying systems, of British India as a 'country' power—an essentially oriental government with strong European overtones—and of traditional India, trembling with unresolved and frequently unstated fears, obsessed with the past and unable or unwilling to accept the modernizing tendencies of the British. The rebellion and the process of its suppression did not itself create the gulf between the Indians and the British, for the reforms of the 1830s and the changing attitude of the administration had already succeeded in alienating the rulers from the many of the ruled. But it did crystallize and reinforce the division by increasing the distrust of both sides.

Apart from inter-racial trust, the most important casualty of the rebellion was the nominal ruler of India, the venerable East India Company, now but a shadow of its founding substance. On 1 November 1858 a proclamation was read at various places throughout India, announcing that the long rule of the Company was over. The pretence of double government was finally at an end. The British Crown now ruled India directly and a new era had come, even if the rebellion was not, as yet, officially over.

The governor-general was at Allahabad. Outside the fort a platform had been raised, covered with a crimson cloth embroidered with the royal arms. On the platform, under a canopy of crimson and gold, stood a richly gilded chair. Lord Canning, attired in court dress and riding a large black horse, was accompanied by military and civil officers in a variety of elegant uniforms, and all were surrounded by Indians wearing scarlet, each carrying a silver wand of office. After a salute of guns, the governor-general—now, in fact, 'viceroy'—ascended the platform and read the long proclamation in English. It was then read in Urdu. More salutes followed, and the viceroy and his staff left the ground. In the evening there was a dinner in the fort, and a display of fireworks.

William Henry Russell, the famous war-correspondent of *The Times* in London, who was present, found the ceremony 'cold and spiritless'. He was told that ordinary Indians had been 'actually prevented or dissuaded from coming to listen to the royal promises of pardon, forgiveness, justice, respect for religious belief, and non-annexation'. It was certainly obvious that 'the natives who were present consisted, for the most part, of officials in the various public offices.'

It was not until July 1859 that Lord Canning was able formally to announce the end of the rebellion. He called for a day of solemn thanksgiving. 'War is at an end; Rebellion has been put down; the Noise of Arms is no longer heard where the enemies of State have persisted in their last struggle; the Presence of large Forces in the Field has ceased to be necessary. Order is re-established; and peaceful Pursuits have everywhere been resumed.'

The words were optimistic but the realities were daunting.

The queen's government had taken over direct responsibility for the government of India, new ideas were in the air, and the problems of reconstruction were immense. Indian finances had been crippled by the rebellion, and the government faced a debt amounting to the then enormous sum of £38 million. The government was also faced with large claims for property destroyed by the rebels or during the operations to suppress them. The revenue-collecting administration had to be reorganized. Above all, the anarchy of the rebellion had ravaged the economic fabric of large parts of northern India.

If only in the interests of future security, the British were anxious to establish not only the causes of the rebellion but the reasons why it had come as such a surprise to the authorities. The solution to the latter question was simple enough, and once arrived at easily remedied—or so the British thought. There would have to be more Englishmen in positions close to the people; only then could the government learn of the people's feelings, their fears and their ambitions.

The causes were more difficult to define, and the number of explanations which had gained currency only made understanding more difficult. Some Englishmen were convinced that English education was at the root of the rebellion. That argument was easily disposed of. The educated classes had not only demonstrated their loyalty to the British, but had openly and strongly condemned the rebels. Some claimed that the rebellion had been sent to chastize the British; Indians had been given all the material benefits of British civilization but not the moral ones.

Others saw, quite clearly, that at least one of the causes had been British interference with long-standing customs and a social organization which had the sanction not only of tradition but of religion. The answer, they believed, was to abandon such interference and to conciliate those who had resented it to the point of revolt. The problem was how to identify the resentful elements. Did they represent specific social classes?

The answer was obviously no, for the rebellion had demonstrated that all classes of Indians, except for the tiny educated
minority, had been divided in their attitude. Very few of the
princes had rebelled, and by no means all of the landholders.
The sepoys—and practically everybody agreed that they had
formed the spearhead of the revolt—had also been divided. In
fact, the British could not have suppressed the rebellion
without the assistance of Indian soldiers and camp-followers.
On the Ridge before Delhi, over half the fighting men had
been Indian, and, as William Howard Russell noted in his
journal, all the other essential supporting tasks had been done
by Indians:

> Look at us here in camp ... Our outposts are native
> troops—natives are cutting grass for and grooming our
> horses, feeding the elephants, managing the transport, sup-
> plying the Commissariat which feeds us, cooking our sol-
> diers' food, cleaning their camp, pitching and carrying their
> tents, waiting on our officers, and even lending us money.
> The soldier who acts as my amanuensis declares his regi-
> ment could not live a week but for the regimental servants,
> dooly-bearers, hospital-men, and other dependants.

At least it was a fairly straightforward matter to reorganize
the native army in such a way that it could never risk mutinying
again. The number of Indian regiments in the Bengal Army
was halved, and the balance of native to white troops reduced
to two to one. This still unavoidable imbalance was corrected
by putting the artillery into exclusively white hands.

The first step in wider reconciliation was a general one. It
was necessary that those who had rebelled should be pardoned
as quickly as possible. Even those found guilty of the murder of
Europeans should be imprisoned rather than executed. Where

property and land had been confiscated, as much as possible should be restored to the owners.

The conservative bias of the government in attaching to itself the landed classes was not allowed to interfere with the modernization of both the administration and the economy. The British had not realized that the modernization process itself was a cause of tension and unease. The Victorian certainty that progress was not only inevitable, but good and desirable, could not be put aside. There was no chance of the government of India becoming either traditional, in the Indian sense, or static. The purpose which justified Britain's imperial rule could not be sustained by inactivity.

There was to be no cessation of the modernizing process itself. But a significant change of attitude did come about. The essential belief which had buttressed earlier policies, that co-operation between the British and the Indian middle classes would produce sweeping reform, was abandoned. A new spirit animated the government, and resulted, as Sir James Fitzjames Stephen, the ideologue of the 'new' India (and uncle of Virginia Woolf) put it, in 'the breakdown of the old system; the renunciation of the attempt to effect an impossible compromise between the Asiatic and the European view of things, legal, military and administrative'.

The British who actually ruled in India, the Civil Service, began to think of themselves as Guardians, men who served the State in the spirit of the defenders of Plato's authoritarian republic. The system they believed in was, paradoxically, both activist and cautious. There was to be no open interference in matters of religion and social custom. But interference there was. Traditional institutions were not destroyed; instead, they were superseded by new systems and allowed to decay. A wide range of archaic institutions therefore survived in parallel with the most advanced. There was no planned substitution of modern economics for traditional ones, but new markets, new techniques, expanding communications, a money-based economy and rapidly fluctuating prices turned traditional India upside down. Yet the British felt that as long as they did not interfere with religion they were safe.

There was no attempt to deny Indians the boons of Western education. On the contrary, at the height of the rebellion, the first universities were established at Calcutta, Bombay and Madras. But the British no longer believed that a Western-educated minority could act as mediator between the majority of Indians and their rulers, that it could be an instrument of modernization. By the end of the nineteenth century, in fact, they were convinced that instead they had created a monster which threatened their rule, and did so in the vocabulary of modern Europe.

But it was not into this peculiarly Eurasian climate of Westernized India that, from the British point of view, the worst of the 'monsters' was to emerge. The princely state of Porbandar, situated on the Kathiawar peninsula which juts out into the Arabian Sea, north-west of Bombay, was remote and to a large extent isolated from the great events and recent passions of Indian history. But it was there that the third son and fourth child of Karamachand and Putlibai Gandhi was born on 2 October 1869.

There was, perhaps, a touch of irony in the fact that it was in the same year that Sir James Fitzjames Stephen was appointed law member of the viceroy's executive council, the cabinet of British India. But then, history, and maybe imperial history especially, is full of ironies.

Part Two

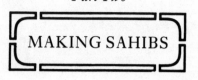

MAKING SAHIBS

4

GREED AND MEGALOMANIA

In the writing of history there is inevitably a gap between rhetoric and reality. After all, as Ernst Toller, the German dramatist and refugee from the Nazis, put it, 'History is the propaganda of the victors. The Raj is no exception. The ideologues, journalists and poets of the high noon of empire produced their elegant and appealing—at least at the time —stories which together make up the "romance of empire".' During the decline of the Raj, and for what seems an unconscionable time after its death, its enemies have produced cruder, but no less appealing distortions of reality.

The best and therefore most effective propaganda—and both the imperialist and anti-imperialist propagandists produced high-quality material—is that which contains the largest percentage of truth. (It would be comparatively simple to produce a surprisingly balanced history of the Raj just by combining the two!) But there are, naturally, irreconcilable differences between the two approaches. Where one sees greed, naked and for the most times unashamed, the other sees enterprise, the entrepreneurial spirit, the sort of get-up-and-go which some Americans today claim to have made, or to be making, America great, and which western Europe— including Britain—would do well to emulate. Where one myopia discerns megalomania and proto-fascist authoritarianism, the other recognizes historical necessity and, above all, *vision*.

Critics of empire can be divided, roughly, into two camps —the liberal and the Marxist. They differ mainly in nuance and on the originality of the sin. But there is no question that they share the opinion that there was something particularly evil about *overseas* colonialism. The reason for this is simple: American and Russian expansion was across an immense land-mass, *towards* the sea, rather than across it.

At the end of the sixteenth century, western Europe was enjoying an economic boom. Prosperity brought demand for luxuries, among them exotic products of Asia, the spices of the Indies, silks from China and Persia and calicoes and indigo from India, as well as drugs and precious stones. England was part of the European economic order, and when that order generated a world-wide trading system, England was part of that, too. It was not a search for export markets for European products and manufactures, but for imports to satisfy the needs of the rich. It used force to keep the price of commodities down at the point of sale, while merchants and rulers competed with every available means to acquire and then maintain a share of the more lucrative trades. There was nothing peaceful about this movement. It was an acquisitive and predatory drive for commodities and for profit in the world outside Europe. In the absence of a land-mass to cross, the Europeans crossed the seas.

The English who crossed the Indian Ocean to Surat in western India and made it their principal place of trade made a wise choice, though it took them some time to establish themselves against the active opposition of their Portuguese rivals already well established down the coast, below Bombay, at Goa, and of local merchants and officials of the Mughal Empire, who found their interests threatened by the new-comers. Force and diplomacy in a varying mixture was used to overcome the resistance. Diplomacy was mainly exercised at the court of the Mughal emperor, in an endeavour to acquire the protection of the central authority against the often arbitary behaviour of its local officials and their merchant friends. The element of force was the growing power of the East India Company's fleet of strong fighting ships, heavily gunned and well manned. In fact, the argument to avoid settlement on land and to pursue well-armed trade at sea was very appealing, especially on the grounds of cost. Forts and soldiers could only be a drain upon profit.

The argument was a wise one, and the Company tried to follow its conclusions. The men who represented the Company on the ground, on the whole concurred. They were interested basically in making a quick profit for themselves as well as their employers, and then getting away to England to enjoy it—if they could, for mortality was heavy. 'Two monsoons are the Age of a Man' was a proverb firmly based upon fact. If 'fluxes, scurvy, barbiers, or the loss of the use of the hands and feet, gout stone, malignant and putrid fevers' did not carry one off, then the treatment for them could do so instead. The fear of disease and death played an important, if somewhat opaque, role in the behaviour of the British in India up until the end of the nineteenth century, when the development of truly preventive treatments began to have some effect. In fact, it seems possible to make a correlation between the decline of the Raj and advances in tropical medicine, as if the psychic climate changed with the prophylactic one.

The eighteenth century, with its drawing of the merchants into the cracks opened by the collapse of the Mughal central authority, enhanced the greed of the British. Originally, it had been only for the profits of trade. To that was now added the probability of plunder. The settlements of the British—little more than collections of traders and sailors at the beginning of the century—became cities made up largely of soldiers. The few military men around in the early trading communities, in Percival Spear's words, 'wished their swords were pens, that they might make money more easily; at the end [of the century] the clerks turned their pens into swords, while merchants converted their bank balances into coronets.' The careers of two strong-minded and ambitious men sum up the change. Almost a hundred years stand between the merchant Thomas

Pitt, governor of the trading station at Madras, and the proconsul, Lord Wellesley, but the gulf is not only that of time. The ambition of Pitt was sealed with the acquisition, by the at best dubious means, of the Pitt diamond, the foundation of the family's political fortune; Wellesley's by the establishment of British supremacy in India.

Naturally, time did not provide a definitive breach between greed and megalomania: personal profit can be almost as easily counted within the psyche as in the pocket-book. Those who gained financial profit from the exercise of the newly found power of the British in India used it for a variety of purposes. Their predecessors, who acquired fortunes as merchants, invested their money in land, as any of their London counterparts who had never left home might have done, and did so without ostentation. But the new men, after Robert Clive's victory at Plassey in 1757, a date which is the putative one for the foundation of British rule in India, expanded their horizons and their desires by venturing outside the purely commercial settlements.

Meeting in the countryside with the local Indian gentry, the new men discovered new levels of wealth and ostentation, luxury and despotic behaviour. They liked what they saw, and took back to England not only the wealth they had amassed, but the desire to be gentlemen, with English titles, to be treated with deference and to enjoy prestige and social distinction. Their pomp and vulgarity soon earned them the name of 'nabobs'—from *nawab*, an Indian princely title.

The nabobs not only used their wealth to acquire political influence in Britain, an influence deeply resented by the establishment, but invested it in new enterprises. Many of these helped to fuel the first Industrial Revolution, which in turn brought profit from India to men who would never set foot in that country. It was these men who first broke the East India Company's trading monopoly in 1813, by getting through the British parliament an Act opening up the India trade to British private enterprise. Before that, British businessmen had been forced to hide behind foreign (Americans being the largest group) and Indian front men.

The opening up of India to unrestricted private enterprise was a disaster for indigenous industry. First to suffer were the hand-loom weavers of Bengal. Indian exports of cotton piece-goods almost ceased after 1815, while imports of machine-made cloth from Lancashire, through private traders, rose very substantially. These imports virtually destroyed the Indian cotton industry, for the hand loom could not compete with the machine, even when that machine was several thousands of miles away.

The growth of private enterprise in India confirmed the division between official and merchant which had been widening ever since the British acquired the respectability of rulers. The greed of the merchant, both individual and corporate, continued, but with a growing element of official control. Exploitation, in the anti-colonialist sense, existed, being the essential concomitant of profit, but the only valid criticism is that the exploitation was on far too limited a scale. Really productive exploitation—productive, that is, in a nation-building sense—would have required immense public investment and close planning direction. For financial and state-of-the-art reasons, neither of these was possible.

Megalomania was more difficult to control, particularly when it manifested itself at the highest levels of the administration. Direct and undivided responsibility for the government of India was not assumed by the British parliament until as late as 1858. Before that, its authority had been exercised only through a governor-general who was appointed by the British cabinet of the time but paid by the trading organization which had made itself ruler of India. But the East India Company's administration was subject to the granting, every few years, of a royal charter. Before 1773, the Company dealt with its affairs in India pretty much as it chose, but a Regulating Act in that year signalled the first attempt of parliament to control the Company and the Company's servants in India. One of the provisions of this Act was the establishment of a Supreme Court in Calcutta designed to administer English law. Its chief purpose, in the words of Edmund Burke, was 'to form a strong and solid security for the natives against the wrongs and oppressions of British subjects resident in Bengal'. Burke's remark, the Act itself, and all the other acts concerning government in India which followed it, represent the continuing division between the legislators and the actual rulers, between the British parliament and the British administrators in India, who worked firstly for the Company and secondly for the Crown.

The British parliament sought, with varying degrees of success, to control its agents in India; Parliament could make laws defining the way in which India *should* be governed, but it could not itself govern India. The reasons for this were simple. In the early days, there was the distance between Britain and India; by the time news reached London from India, the authorities in India had already acted. The British government could only confirm or condemn the *fait accompli*. As communications improved, however, with the opening of the telegraph between India and Britain in 1865 and of the Suez Canal in 1869, the control exercised by the secretary of state over his representative, the viceroy, increased according to the strength of personality of the two men involved. Nevertheless, the secretary of state in London could not control the actual everyday administration of India at any time. India was too big and the volume of administrative business too vast for the constant approval of a cabinet minister thousands of miles away. The British government, and through it the British parliament, controlled only the general policy of Indian administration; it could not direct its application in practice.

The introduction, in the twentieth century, of such rapid means of communication as the radio and the aeroplane, brought the cabinet in London closer to the decision-making process in New Delhi. But a stronger inhibition to the continuing exercise of what might be called a 'creative' megalomania was the growing challenge to British rule *inside* India. A colonial regime under internal threat has only two choices if it is to survive: to display unflinchingly the crudities of power, or to be cautious and conservative. On the whole the British chose the latter, and, in doing so, found an unexpected, if unpredictable, ally in the leader of the opposition.

5

CARE AND CONCERN

The British, through the years of their imperial power had
—and still have—a healthy suspicion of intellectuals, especially so should they achieve positions of political influence. Yet
the British found success in conquering India going to their
heads. In the first half of the nineteenth century, this most
unideological of peoples produced no less than three separate,
though linked, sets of ideas about how to deal with the vast,
populous and alien territories they now ruled: the religious, the
romantic-pragmatist, and the utilitarian. All three contained
an essential element—care and concern for the generality of
the Indian people and, in particular, for the poor. Two of the
three also shared a common aim, combining both grandeur
and grandiosity. The religious and the utilitarian sought to
transform Indian society by an exercise in social engineering,
comparable in conception with the 'cultural revolution' of Mao
Zedong in China, more than a century later.

When the British came to exercise power in Bengal, they
were faced with a series of dilemmas. The first was how to rule
without revealing that the British had neither the capacity nor
the manpower to operate an administration. Robert Clive's
notorious system of 'dual government' was the first solution to
be tried. The native administration and its officials continued
to function, while the British remained in the background.
This was primarily a matter of expediency, but what was, in
essence, a puppet system also appealed to the British because
their main interest was in profit. They considered themselves
not as innovators, but as inheritors, and they hoped to make
their inheritance work for them. They thought of themselves

not as colonists, but as transients, making their fortune before climate and disease prevented them from enjoying it back home in Britain. They were content to adapt themselves to Indian circumstances and to manipulate the traditional forms of government. Nevertheless, the very presence of the British in the Indian countryside, as well as their use of traditional forms to their own advantage, influenced the system of administration. And as the numbers of British increased, so did the influence. It was to curtail their predatory activities that the Crown first decided to interfere in the administration of British India.

When dual government was abandoned in 1772, the British were faced with their second dilemma. To what extent should the government be anglicized? Were existing institutions to be preserved, or swept aside? Warren Hastings felt that Indian institutions should be retained wherever possible. During his administration, Hindu and Muslim personal law received protection, Muslim criminal law was maintained, and Indians were employed in the administration. In effect, the principle of duality was continued, except that now it was operated directly by the British—who were themselves subject to English law, as exercised by the new Supreme Court set up by the Regulating Act of 1773.

It was hardly to be expected that the introduction of direct rule would completely eradicate abuse and corruption, and when Hastings's successor, Lord Cornwallis, arrived in India in 1786, he soon became convinced that there was not enough control exercised over the Company's servants.

The Supreme Court had been established with the intention of making individuals subject to English law; Cornwallis decided that English constitutional principles should form the basis of the system of government. In Cornwallis's view, these principles were entirely opposed to the authoritarian character of native Indian government. His purpose was to establish the rule of law instead of the law of the ruler—to provide something fixed and immutable in place of something variable and arbitrary. The corruption and misery of Bengal were, Cornwallis believed, the result of allowing too much discretion to underpaid Company servants, who fell easily into the ways of native Indian governments. Cornwallis's solution was to reduce the role of government. He opted for 'the introduction of a new order of things, which should have for its foundation, the security of Indian property, and the administration of justice, criminal and civil, by rules which were to disregard all conditions of persons, and in their operation, be free of influence or control from the government itself'.

The question of land revenue provided full scope for putting these views into action. Cornwallis ruled that the amount payable to the government should be permanently fixed, thus limiting interference by officials which, Cornwallis believed, took place when the revenue demand varied from year to year. One of the essential bases of Cornwallis's ideas was that the executive should be separated from the judiciary, and that the executive itself should be subject to the rule of law. This was a revolutionary suggestion, not only for Indians, but for the British in India who, following Indian practice, had made no division between the authority which made the law and the authority which enforced it. Even the men who collected the revenue possessed judicial powers. Cornwallis proposed to put an end to this. In his preamble to Bengal Regulation II of 1793, he wrote:

The collectors of revenue must not only be divested of the power of deciding upon their own acts, but rendered amenable for them to the courts of judicature; and collect the public dues, subject to a personal prosecution for every exaction exceeding the amount which they are authorized to demand on behalf of the public, and for every deviation from the regulations prescribed for the collection of it.

[54]

Like the good Whig he was, Cornwallis believed that the prosperity of the State rested on landed property, and his purpose was to see that this principle was irrevocably established in British India.

English political concepts were to be transplanted into the soil of India, and Indians were to be removed from the halls of government. With Cornwallis's admiration for English principles and institutions went a belief in the general superiority of Englishmen and the role they must play in preserving British rule in India. 'I think it must be universally admitted', he wrote, 'that without a large and well-regulated body of Europeans, our hold on these valuable dominions must be very insecure.' Indians were dismissed from all but the most minor offices. In Bengal, landowners who had had the right to employ armed retainers—and who were responsible for policing their districts—were deprived of this right. A British official, known as the collector, was appointed to each administrative area in Bengal with the task of collecting the revenue. He had no political or judicial powers. Such powers were to be exercised by the man known as district judge and magistrate, who controlled the police and whose function was to administer the law, even against the collector, if necessary.

Although the principle of separation of powers involved conscious anglicization of the forms of government, it was not intended to change Indian society. On the contrary, supporters of the principle—particularly Lord Wellesley (governor-general 1798–1805)—believed that in it lay the best protection for that society. Wellesley argued that the interests of the mass of the people were non-political, involving no principles of government. If the government refrained from interference in religion, customs and personal law, Indian society could maintain its domestic structure. But whatever Wellesley might believe, interference there was. The British concept of private-property rights and their enforcement by legal process was a radical innovation, and its effects were to alter the structure of Indian society profoundly.

If the ideas of Cornwallis and Wellesley may be said to have had their roots in the Whig view of society, classically stated by John Locke, the ideas of the opposition stemmed from romantic sentiments about the 'noble peasant' as expounded by William Wordsworth. This did not, however, mean that the men of the opposition such as Thomas Munro (1761–1827), John Malcolm (1769–1833), Mountstuart Elphinstone (1779–1859) and Charles Metcalfe (1785–1846)—from whose thoughts and actions emerged an alternative to anglicized forms of government—were sloppy sentimentalists; far from it. They believed in pragmatic, personal and dynamic administration, free from the dead hand of impersonal government. While they did not deny that English constitutional principles were intrinsically good, they doubted their relevance to the Indian situation unless modified in their application.

The importance of these four particular men was that they were not abstract thinkers but active administrators who, because the frontiers of British India were still expanding, were able to exercise considerable authority independently of the government in Calcutta. The Bengal system—by now a settled administration in an area where British rule was undisputed—had become cold and passive. Inherently, it was a system of division, above all of rejection, for its purpose was to avoid involvement in the lives of the people. To men actively engaged in empire-building beyond such settled territories, the system lacked both warmth and what might be called the bravura of involvement. They were by no means opposed to reform, but they could not accept the belief that miraculous changes could be wrought in human society merely by means of legislative action. To them, a division of society between ruler and ruled was the natural order, and they believed in the exercise of political power as of right.

Munro, Malcolm, Elphinstone and Metcalfe differed on

[56]

points of detail, particularly in their attitude to native states and to the old aristocracy. Munro believed it to be good policy to conciliate the princes and others. Metcalfe was against it. But none of them expected that British rule would ever rest upon the affection of the masses. Their common aim was not to engage in some vast operation designed to transform the Indian subcontinent into a vague simulacrum of British society, but to conserve traditional institutions. They were against innovation and fully aware of what its effects had been in Cornwallis's time. When a new move towards increased anglicization began in the 1820s, they feared the worst. 'The ruling vice of our government', wrote Munro in 1824, 'is innovation . . . It is time that we should learn that neither the face of the country, its property, nor its society are things that can be suddenly improved by any contrivance of ours, though they may be greatly injured by what we mean for their good.'

In spite of their superficial disagreements, Munro, Malcolm, Elphinstone and Metcalfe were preservationists. Except for Metcalfe—whose outlook had been soured by direct experience of dealing with Maratha princes—they believed that the Indian states should be preserved, not only as places where Indian culture could survive in the most natural milieu, but also as a refuge for those Indians who could find no place in the hierarchies of British India. A direct relationship between the ruler and the ruled was, they argued, the foundation of stability. There should be ease of access between government and peasant—government by mouth rather than by pen, instant decision rather than a multiplicity of written forms and slow judicial processes. This, in practice, demanded not the separation of judicial and executive powers but their union. The four administrators considered that the collector should have magisterial authority, control of the police, and, above all, the power to impose summary punishment. Although convinced of the need for efficiency and economy in government, they felt it would be better achieved by delegating authority to trusted individuals surrounded by the realities of everyday life than by a centralized and therefore remote administration. In essence, Munro, Malcolm, Elphinstone and Metcalfe were in agreement with certain of the views of English utilitarian philosophers, who also believed in the union of judicial and executive powers, in a simple code of law and respect for custom. But they could not accept either the desire for uniformity or the rigidity of principle involved in the utilitarian outlook.

Above all, the romantic school of Indian administrators in the first half of the nineteenth century were fearful of violent change. John Malcolm wrote:

> The most important lesson we can derive from past experience is to be slow and cautious in every procedure which has a tendency to collision with the habits and prejudices of our native subjects. We may be compelled by the character of our government to frame some institutions, different from those we found established, but we should adopt all we can of the latter into our system . . . Our internal government . . . should be administered on a principle of humility not pride. We must divest our minds of all arrogant pretensions arising from the presumed superiority of our own knowledge, and seek the accomplishment of the great ends we have in view by the means which are best suited to the peculiar nature of the objects . . . All that Government can do is, by maintaining the internal peace of the country, and by adapting its principles to the various feelings, habits, and character of its inhabitants, to give time for the slow and silent operation of the desired improvement, with a constant impression that every attempt to accelerate this end will be attended with the danger of its defeat.

Essentially, the systems of Cornwallis and of Munro (and those who thought like him) were to prove permanent in the different parts of the country in which they were established by their creators. The general structure of both systems remained untouched, although there were to be many modifications and sometimes violent change within the structures. Both systems were designed to limit governmental interference in society, but both were designed to be operated by British officials, and both imposed Western concepts of property rights backed by Western law. The control of the administration by British officials meant that those officials could become agents of revolution if the climate of opinion in British India, or in Britain, changed. And the effect of Western legal institutions on matters concerning land—the core of Indian society— could be used as an instrument to transform that society.

Cornwallis's attitude—which involved the removal of Indians from positions of authority and the rejection of traditional administrative forms—was grounded fundamentally in a sense of racial superiority and its corollary, contempt for others. As the British in India ceased to be merchants and became empire-builders, they acquired a strong sense of exclusivity, occupying that special isolation which is characteristic of all conquerors. This was reinforced by a growing belief, not only that the British were racially superior to Indians and possessed of infinitely better political institutions, but that their religion was superior too. This assumption would not have meant very much if it had not been intimately associated with missionary zeal on the part of a number of people with influence in Indian affairs. The most important of these was Charles Grant, who had been one of Cornwallis's advisers in India and who, after his return to England, became chairman of the Court of Directors of the East India Company. His view, which illuminates the new mission that he and his associates proposed for Christianity, he summed up in these words:

In considering the affairs of the world as under the control of the Supreme Disposer, and those distant territories i.e.

India providentially put into our hands . . . is it not necessary
to conclude that they were given to us, not merely that we
might draw an annual profit from them, but that we might
diffuse among their inhabitants, long sunk in darkness, vice
and misery, the light and benign influence of the truth, the
blessings of well-regulated society, the improvements and
comforts of active industry? . . . In every progressive step of
this work, we shall also serve the original design with which
we visited India, that design still so important to this country
—the extension of our commerce.

The evangelicals—as Grant and his friends, who included
William Wilberforce and the father of the future Lord
Macaulay, were called—dismissed not only the religions of
India as 'one grand abomination', but also by implication every
aspect of Indian society, from its arts to its institutions. Except
in one area however, these views had very little effect upon the
Company's administration, because the evangelicals believed
that society could not be reformed by legislation, but only by a
change in individual morality. They intended a campaign to
free the Indian mind from the tyranny of evil superstition, a sort
of Indian counterpart to the European Reformation. Their
instrument was to be education, for only through access to
God's revealed word could the Indians be raised out of their
darkness and idolatry.

The evangelicals believed that the future prosperity of the
British connection and the future happiness of the Indians
themselves depended upon the complete anglicization of
Indian society. 'Let us endeavour to strike our roots into the
soil', said Wilberforce, 'by the gradual introduction and establishment of our own principles and opinions; of our laws,
institutions, and manners; above all, as the source of every
other improvement, of our religion, and consequently of our
morals.'

This view represented a real challenge to the East India

Company's continuing attitude of non-interference. The British in India, though conscious of their power, were equally conscious that it depended on the acceptance of the large mass of people who did not particularly care who governed them as long as their customs and religion were not interfered with. Any attempt to convert Indians to Christianity promised to subvert the very foundations of civil peace by offending the most deeply entrenched religious prejudices. The Company's administration had endeavoured to maintain a sense of continuity with the past, to emphasize that, though it was an alien administration, it contemplated no revolutionary changes in the lives of the people. The truth of this was most apparent to Indians in that very area attacked by the evangelicals, namely the Company's religious policy.

This policy was essentially concerned with not giving offence, and it was taken to such lengths that, until 1831, Indian Christians were actively discriminated against by the government. They could not hold appointments in the Company's judicial service, nor were they permitted to practise as lawyers in the Company's courts. In contrast, the government not only tolerated Hindu and Muslim festivals but allowed troops and military bands to participate in them. In 1802, for example, as a thanksgiving for the conclusion of the Treaty of Amiens between Britain and France, an official government party went in procession with troops and military music to the principal shrine of the Hindu goddess, Kali, in Calcutta, and presented the goddess with a substantial sum of money.

The British had also assumed certain of the responsibilities of previous governments in relation to religious endowments and buildings and the control of pilgrim traffic to the many Hindu shrines. The issue of a Regulation in 1817 was followed by government administration of a large number of temples and their funds. The pilgrim taxes levied by the Company were used for the repair and upkeep of temples. In fact, the government's involvement left its servants wide open to the criticism

[61]

of supporting idolatry and acting, in the picturesque language of one observer, as 'dry-nurse to Vishnu'. As late as 1833, the Madras government was still responsible for the administration of some 7,500 temples and their funds. British officials played an intimate role in the material life of the temples —assessing and ordering repairs, and even, on occasion, press-ganging men to pull the temple cars.

The Charter Act of 1833 was to change this, though many years passed before it took effect and it was not until 1863 that the government finally severed its connection with the administration of religious endowments. Many Indians were to look upon this ultimate dissociation of the government from involvement in the administration of temples and their funds —an involvement which was a traditional function of India's rulers—as an abdication of one of the principal functions of government, and a deliberate repudiation of a duty incumbent upon all rulers, whatever religion they professed. More important still, it was to appear as yet another act of withdrawal, separating the government from the people and dramatizing for Indian society the uniquely alien nature of British government in India.

The evangelicals had their first triumph in 1813 when, by the Charter Act of that year, the Company was forced to appoint a bishop whose headquarters were to be in Calcutta and his see the whole of the British dominions; to open up the country to Christian missionaries; and to appropriate an annual sum for education. The Charter Act of 1813 also forced open the door of the Company's commercial monopoly, although many evangelicals were, like Charles Grant, staunch supporters of a Company monopoly. Most of them possessed a vested interest in its maintenance, and ironically enough, believed they could reform the government of India without impinging upon the mercantilist conception of political dominion, which saw its *raison d'être* as the drawing-off of tribute. The rational extension of their view, which can be briefly summed up as 'assimilation and profit', was, in fact, free trade, colonization and capital investment—not the drawing away of wealth, but the creation of prosperity. The Company, however, was already an anachronism as a trading corporation. Ever since its occupation of Bengal after 1757, trade had taken a low second place to revenue control and the transformation of revenue surplus into dividends for the Company's stock-holders back in Britain. But the expansion of British dominion in India soon produced a burden of debt instead of a revenue surplus. By 1813, the Company had become basically a military and administrative power. It paid its way by using the profits of the opium monopoly in India to finance trade in China tea—from whose sale in Europe the shareholders' dividends were paid. Nevertheless, the Company resisted the breaking of its monopoly in the India trade, primarily on the grounds that free trade would lead to attempts to 'improve' Indian conditions and this would, it believed, endanger internal stability. In any case, it was convinced that no sudden improvement was possible.

The Company's attitude, however, ran counter to the spirit of the times, and, by the time the charter came up for renewal in 1833, evangelical opinion coincided with that of the free traders. By then, the evangelicals had witnessed some years of attempted improvement and social reform in India. The free traders had also gained an insight into India's profitability; the Company had lost its trading monopoly (except that with China) in 1813, and the extent of private trade—particularly in manufactured cotton textiles—had amply justified the hopes of the free traders. But their very success raised doubts about the future. Indians were poor and their purchasing power was strictly limited. If this were to be changed, it would necessitate the widest use of British expertise as well as considerable financial investment. Such a programme would call for the abolition of restrictions on European ownership of land and of discriminatory inland transit dues.

All this could be achieved—and was achieved—by political lobbying in Britain. But the creed of the apostles of free trade embraced more than the expansion of commerce. They firmly believed that the Industrial Revolution which was investing Britain with the commercial leadership of the world resulted from a superior civilization, and the passing-on of its benefits was not only good business but a heaven-ordained duty. The only way this could be carried out was by spreading English institutions and English education. One of the results was that a Law Commission was appointed to codify Indian law according to Western principles. Another was that, in 1835, it was decided that English education in the English language should receive the principal support of the government of India. Essentially this denoted a *mission civilisatrice* rather than a philosophy of conquest. As Macaulay said: 'To trade with civilized men is infinitely more profitable than to govern savages.'

Paradoxical though it may appear, evangelicals and liberals such as Macaulay still wished to restrict government interference in the everyday life of the people of India. They believed that it was the government's duty to create a climate of change—but not to bully people into changing; to offer the means of change—but a means suitably protected by a hedge of English institutions; to persuade by example—but not to coerce by legislative action. They believed, however, that the government should be unmistakably British, demonstrating that its superiority stemmed from its civilization. Indeed, the general movement towards anglicization was aimed as much at the government of India as at Indian society. While legislation in London could be used to change the government's attitude, Indian society was expected to transform itself as knowledge of Western civilization was diffused by English education.

There were other thinkers who did not agree with the propositions of the evangelicals and the liberals, who had little faith in the regenerative qualities of English education and who saw very clearly that the *real* instrument by which a radical transformation of Indian society could be achieved was the system of land revenue, its determination and assessment. Some of these men—generally called utilitarians—were in a position to influence India's administration. James Mill, for example, had been appointed to a senior post in the East India Company's headquarters in London in 1819; in 1830, he became the examiner, or chief executive officer. Jeremy Bentham was the intellectual *animateur* of Lord William Bentinck, the reforming governor-general (1828–35). William Empson, a confirmed Benthamite, was professor of General Polity and Laws at the Company's college at Haileybury, where its administrators received their initial training. Although none of the principal utilitarian philosophers had any personal experience in India, they knew instinctively that it was quite as bad as, if not worse than, the descriptions of Charles Grant. James Mill, comparing India with China (which he also knew only at second hand), found that

> both nations are, to nearly an equal degree, tainted with the vices of insincerity; dissembling, treacherous, mendacious, to an excess which surpasses even the usual measure of uncultivated society. Both are disposed to excessive exaggeration with regard to everything relating to themselves. Both are cowardly and unfeeling. Both are in the highest degree conceited of themselves, and full of affected contempt for others. Both are, in the physical sense, disgustingly unclean in their persons and their houses.

Both the evangelicals and utilitarians shared a fundamental contempt for Indian institutions, a contempt which became institutionalized as the nineteenth century progressed. But they shared little else. The difference between them lay in their concept of the operative law. The evangelicals believed in God's law, immutable and evident. In their view, all that was needed was to make knowledge of this law available to all; example could then be expected to do the rest. The utilitarians expelled God from the equation. To them, sin was not original but a product of poverty; and poverty was—wrote James Mill—'the effect of bad laws and bad government; and is never characteristic of any people who are governed well'. Mill had no faith in schoolmasters as purveyors of revolution. That savoured of placing the cart before the horse. 'It is necessary,' he went on, 'before education can operate to any great result, that the poverty of the people be re-dressed; that their laws and government should operate beneficently.'

This was a cold and mechanist view of social change, and one which did not appeal to the messianism of the new English middle class. For one thing, it did not support their essentially patriotic view of the value of British civilization. Mill and the economist Ricardo even threw doubt on the fundamental belief that free trade was the creator of happiness. What was even worse—at least from the point of view of the British mercantile community in India—was that Mill disapproved of the Cornwallis system which restricted the executive authority of government and relied on purely conservative application of the law to protect private property.

In the case of the law itself, Bentham opposed the jury system and glorified summary procedures. Mill believed that, in the Indian interior, both British and Indians should be subject to the same laws and the same courts. As well as offending the deep-seated prejudices of the mercantile community, the utilitarians repelled the liberals who believed that Indians should play a part in the administration of their own country. Mill argued that the people of India wanted cheap and efficient government and did not really care who operated it as long as these criteria were satisfied. He rejected the idea even of a legislature representing the British in India. Mill's remedy for India's ills was quite simple:

[66]

The mode of increasing the riches of the body of the people is a discovery no less easy than sure. Take little from them in the way of taxes; prevent them from injuring one another; and make no absurd laws to restrain them in the harmless disposal of their property and labour. Light taxes and good laws; nothing more is wanting for national and individual prosperity all over the globe.

It was an essential of Mill's thesis that, as in Munro's system, there should be no middlemen between the State and the actual cultivator of the land. But he also called for a code of law which would be universal in its application and mode of procedure; even more important, for a strong central authority; and for an end to the semi-independent status of the Madras and Bombay presidencies.

At the heart of the utilitarian theories about India, however, lay the question of land revenue. Every level of Indian society, outside the urban areas, depended in one way or another upon the land. Before the fundamental rights of a rural community could be protected by the law, these rights had to be determined and recorded—a procedure which could be satisfactorily achieved only by means of Munro's system, in which the administration had a direct and unimpeded relationship with the cultivators of the soil. But of even more importance than the definition of rights was the method of taxation which, according to Mill, was one of the great forces that in conjunction with the form of government and the administration of justice moulded all human society.

Mill maintained that the State was, in effect, the universal landlord. This view was supported by Indian tradition, but was also a rebuttal of both the Cornwallis and the Munro systems, which sought by implication to remove the State from that position. The problem, as Mill saw it, was to determine the rent payable to the universal landlord. In its correct setting, i.e. the general chaos of Indian circumstances, Mill's apparently simple solution to the country's ills appears in its true light as a vast programme of reform. It entailed the establishment of a strong central government possessing exclusive legislative authority for the whole of British India; the embodiment of all law into a set of scientific codes; a total reorganization and expansion of the judicial system; a complete overhaul and reshaping of the administrative service; the survey and registration of all landholdings; and a scientific assessment of land revenue based on detailed statistics of agricultural production. Yet, over a period of many years, and certainly not in its pure form, Mill's programme was actually carried through. It was to be diluted partly for environmental reasons and partly because the coldness of utilitarian ideas did not appeal to the liberal modernizers who were to carry out administrative and judicial reforms in India.

The real effect of utilitarian ideas during the period of Company rule depended upon two factors—Mill's position as a senior official of the Company in London, and the activities of certain men in India who had been converted to utilitarian principles. By the time James Mill gave evidence before a parliamentary committee in 1831, he was able to reveal that, for many years, instructions from London concerning the amount of the revenue assessment had stipulated that it should be restricted to the limits of the net produce, i.e. the surplus after the payment of wage-labour and the natural profits of capital, which the utilitarians called 'rent'. Mill also revealed, however, that there had been and still were immense difficulties involved in ascertaining rent and that, although this was partly due to the absence of statistics, the main difficulty lay in the fact that the revenue administrators themselves did not understand Mill's 'doctrine of rent'. But there was at least one person in a position of authority in India who did: the secretary to the Supreme Government in the Territorial Department in Calcutta, one Holt Mackenzie. Mackenzie had produced a memorandum in 1819 outlining a new system of land settlement for those areas in northern and central India which were later to be called the North-Western Provinces. Although the governor-general accepted the system in 1822, the Regulation embodying it was in practice largely ignored because of the difficulty of estimating the proceeds and expenses of cultivation. Local custom operated such a bewildering series of restrictive practices—including price-fixing—that the law of supply and demand did not exist.

There was opposition to the new system. John Malcolm considered it too academic, ignoring reality because it was too concerned with rigid principles. An assessment based on net produce was, in fact, carried out in Bombay in 1828, but in spite of (or even, perhaps, because of) its detailed statistical framework, it was generally considered—though not by Mill and the directors in London—as too high. The assessment was abandoned in 1835. In general, after 1833, another less doctrinaire and far more empirical method of revenue assessment came into favour.

The failure of utilitarian methods of revenue assessment was almost entirely due to the inadequacy of the administration. The searching investigation and detailed statistics necessary if these methods were to operate properly demanded more men—and more qualified men—than the administration possessed. Theoretically, however, the net-produce criterion was never abandoned, though it was considerably altered in practice.

In their effect on society, perhaps the most important aspect of Mill's views and their embodiment in the revenue system of northern and western India was that they had an essentially anti-landlord bias. Indeed, in the North-Western Provinces, discrimination against the landlord—or, as the utilitarians called him, the rent receiver—and the upheaval this caused in the social order, helped to bring about civil involvement in the essentially military Mutiny of 1857.

The concept of private-property rights and their alienation

[69]

for debt lay at the heart of every Western system—whether it was that of Cornwallis, Munro or the utilitarians—and it was this that was to dissolve the traditional social order. The moment land acquired realizable value either in outright sale or as security for loans, any tradition of communal inter-dependence as exemplified by joint proprietorship or co-sharing village-owned land tended to be eroded. There was a movement towards individual ownership supported, through the proper registration of title, by precise and legally enforce-able definition instead of unwritten and therefore legally unen-forceable custom.

This affected the whole of British India. But there was no uniformity in the matter of assessment or in the definition of land tenures. Before 1858, too much depended on the indi-vidual preferences of local administrators bound only by the Company's general instruction to maintain a moderate assess-ment. In a real sense, India was a series of laboratories for experiments in political economy.

The movement towards codification of the law was slow, principally because after 1835 the British were engaged in a succession of wars both inside and outside India which left successive governors-general with little time—and, fre-quently, less inclination—for contemplating major reforms.

There remained Mill's third reform, a strong central gov-ernment. There was an essential conflict between the two systems of government operating in India, whose leading protagonists were Cornwallis and Munro. This lay in the question of the separation of powers. The paternalist school, represented by Munro, Malcolm, Elphinstone and Metcalfe, believed implicitly that executive and judicial functions should be combined. So did Mill and Bentham, although not for the same reasons. To the paternalists, the union of these powers —and a wide discretion for the officials actually operating them—was a preservationist link with traditional Indian prac-tice. To the utilitarians, the union of these powers was a matter

[70]

of simple and rational common sense. That both attitudes were compatible was demonstrated in Elphinstone's administration of Bombay (1819–27), when he followed the Munro system but underwrote it with a precise and careful delegation of authority. Elphinstone also attempted to codify Hindu law, but ultimately had to be content with producing a consistent system of English law.

Widespread administrative reform, however, had to await the arrival in India in 1828 of Lord William Bentinck. His instructions were to try to put the Company's administration into some sort of order in preparation for 1833, when the Company's charter came up for renewal. There was a substantial annual budget deficit, and it had been obvious for some time that the civil administration was, to put it charitably, less than efficient. In certain parts of the country, in fact, administrative collapse seemed imminent. This was a result of the absence of knowledgeable supervision. In the North-Western Provinces, for example, the provincial boards of revenue were expected to exercise control over the district revenue administration by means of correspondence. They were unable to do so.

Before Bentinck's arrival, a suggestion had been put forward in India that new officials should be appointed, each of whom would be given full responsibility in a district of manageable size where he could keep a personal eye on the activities of his subordinates. These officials—district commissioners, as they came to be called—were, in turn, to be accountable for everything that went on in their districts. They were to be not executives, but inspectors. Both the utilitarians and the paternalists believed in personal government at the level of action, carried on by experienced and practical men linked to higher authority by a precise chain of command. The plan for district commissioners, responsible individuals operating within an area in which inspection and control could effectively be exercised, conformed excellently with utilitarian and paternalistic ideas.

In 1829, the plan was put into action in the Bengal Presidency. The boards of revenue were replaced by the new commissioners, who took over control of the police and also became judges of circuit and session. A chief board of revenue was formed at Calcutta to act as the highest controlling authority.

In Bengal, the commissioners exercised judicial functions only in matters concerning land revenue, but, as the system spread elsewhere, the union of powers desired by both utilitarians and paternalists was achieved. In time, the commissioner system spread throughout the whole of Britain's colonial Empire. What had begun with Bentinck's Regulation I of 1829 as a method designed (except in the initial case of Bengal) to facilitate immediate control of newly acquired territories in India became the orthodox pattern of colonial government.

These changes in the executive arm of the government also made possible reforms in the administration of justice—a matter of some urgency, since the courts were clogged with arrears. But the movement towards reform once again aroused the controversy over the functions of the executive power and the rule of law as instruments of social change. In the minds of the paternalists, orthodox utilitarians and liberals, the mechanics of government and the social purposes of governmental action were inseparable. The ideas of administration propounded in both Britain and India were concerned with wider matters than producing cheap and efficient administration as such, or even than erecting a system which could collect the maximum revenue in the most expeditious fashion. Some thinkers and administrators in India insisted that the function of government was to protect and preserve. Others believed that social change should be brought about by executive action. Others, again, were convinced that the rule of law itself, by its efficient operation, would naturally bring into being an individualist, competitive society such as had given Britain her dominating position in the world.

Bentinck succeeded in achieving the increased administrative efficiency which had been his brief on appointment. But there remained one overwhelming problem. This was not so much the very obvious lack of uniformity between different parts of the British dominions as the inability of the governor-general to impose uniformity. The governor-general's field of authority—and that of the presidency governments—had been fixed by the British parliament and could only be changed by it. It was clear to most people that, lacking any single legislative authority, the government of India was in confusion. This situation, and the absence of a single system of law, resulted in the major provisions of the Charter Act of 1833, which created a real government of India, complete with legislative council.

Reform in the government of India was brought about in the face of powerful but essentially helpless opposition. The paternalists were naturally opposed to the concentration of power at the centre and a uniform administration for the whole of British India. They favoured *delegation* of authority and wide discretionary powers for local officials. There was, they agreed, a need for administrative and legal reform. They believed, however, that codification, for example, should be pursued with intent to provide not only a uniform law throughout India but a series of comprehensive bodies of law designed to protect local rights and customs from the alien and disruptive effect of English law. The paternalists were convinced that local experiments in administration were infinitely better than all-India uniformity. But their views ran counter to the general feeling of the time.

Other opposition centred on the composition of the legislative council. Most opinion in India favoured a body with some popular basis, one which might include not only the members of the governor-general's executive council, two judges, and representatives of the presidencies, but also possibly a number of 'unofficial native gentlemen'. This dimly democratic concept ran counter to all utilitarian principles. Mill maintained that a small body of experts was prefereable on grounds of efficiency, and also argued that it would be more amenable to the influences of public opinion. Essentially, however, his view was that the business of government should be left to specialists who were not encumbered by the passions of what Bentham called 'the untaught and unlettered multitude'. Though Mill did not get exactly what he wanted, the Charter Act did accept the principle of small bodies of experts when it established the Law Commission, of four members.

The first man to occupy the position of law member was Thomas Babington Macaulay. Unlike the utilitarians, he professed no general theories of government. His mind was essentially practical. He rejected the utilitarian belief that society could be changed by the exercise of a universally applicable theory. He retained the old Whig suspicion of political power but, true to his times, accepted a large role for the State in the pursuit of limited aims. Macaulay believed that free enterprise and voluntary action were the springs of progress, and he was therefore strongly opposed to the authoritarian elements in the utilitarian ideal. Nevertheless, although he consciously rejected utilitarian principles, he had assimilated many of the practical attitudes of utilitarian political science. To Macaulay, reform of the law was a rational and immediate objective, a matter of efficiency rather than of social engineering in the interests of fundamental improvement in Indian character and society. In effect, Macaulay's arrival in India removed the threat to the Cornwallis system of minimum interference, for his aim was to recondition, not to destroy.

Utilitarian theorists believed that legislation should be simply expressed and that 'public opinion' should be made aware of the reasons behind the law. Bentham maintained that the best way of limiting abuse of power by the executive was to give the widest possible publicity to these reasons. Macaulay supported this view. It was particularly important in India to explain the reasons for legislation, he said, because India was

> perhaps the only country in the world where the press is free while the government is despotic. In all other despotic States, writers are afraid to criticise public measures with severity. In all other States where free political discussion is allowed, there is some public assembly in which the authors of laws have an opportunity of vindicating those laws. If the emperor of Russia puts forth an ukase, no Russian writes about it except to defend it. If an English or French minister brings forward a law, he has an opportunity of arguing for it in Parliament or in the Chambers, and his arguments are read by hundreds of thousands within a few hours after they have been uttered. We [the British in India] are perhaps the only rulers in the world who are mute on political questions, while all our subjects are unmuzzled. Our laws are the only laws which are exposed naked and undefended to the attacks of a free press.

Though Macaulay's point was a good one, the Press in India at this time was almost entirely European-owned and in the English language. Generally speaking, it reflected only the entrenched interests of the British community. The 'public opinion' which was in any way influenced by the Press was that of an extremely small minority, and it was certainly not *Indian* public opinion except in the case of the few Indians who could read English.

It was, however, decided that, when legislation had passed into law, it should be translated into a number of Indian languages. This, of course, was 'for information only'. There was no real question of inviting public criticism of proposed legislation before it was passed; *draft* legislation was to be published only in English. The views of the governor-general-in-council were succinctly expressed in a letter, sent to the government of Bengal, outlining the method of publicizing legislation.

> It would seem also advisable that the drafts of Acts should be made known to the native community before they are passed into law by which means the Governor-General-in-Council doubts not that many valuable suggestions might be offered to Government; but his Lordship in Council apprehends that this object could not be attained except by the sacrifice of much time, for it is obvious that the ordinary period of six weeks' notice would be far from sufficient for this purpose. There may besides be other objections in the present state of society to invite the opinions of the entire native community of the legislative projects of Government.

Efficiency was the watchword, and though there are indications that Macaulay himself would have liked to consult a much wider spectrum of public opinion, it was certainly quite impractical to do so without some machinery for surveying that opinion.

By 1838, the age of reform in India was over. After Bentinck's departure in 1835, little progress was made. The government—as one writer lamented in the *Edinburgh Review* in 1841—was so preoccupied with external problems that it had 'no adequate leisure for civil concerns of the utmost importance to the happiness of millions'. But there was more to it than just preoccupation on the part of the government of India. As the intellectual climate had earlier created a desire for reform in India, so a change in that climate brought about a change of attitude. When James Mill died in 1836, there died with him the eighteenth-century belief in man's perfectability and the power of political institutions to produce it. The Victorians were not quite so sure of themselves, nor quite so ambitious to change the world overnight. Certainly, they were optimistic. But they were cautious, too.

The utilitarian ideal, however, did not vanish into limbo in India. In Sind (annexed 1842) and the Punjab (finally absorbed in 1849), the form of government used was very close to the pattern of Bentham and Mill. There was no division beween executive and judiciary. A highly disciplined body of men ruled the country. The Punjab administration was planned on military lines and, though in terms of executive strategy the man on the spot had discretion to act, his actions could be appealed against to higher authority. To ensure the validity of this right to appeal, each officer had to keep records, and any case sent for higher decision resulted in a demand for a personal report on the officer's part. The district officer was also subject to inspection. The Punjab system, in fact, had its origins in the methods used by Charles Metcalfe—a paternalist by conviction—when he administered the newly acquired Delhi territory in 1811–19 and 1825–7. But the Punjab system was not a resurrected paternalism, although the men who operated it have often been shown, particularly by nineteenth-century British historians and their followers, as almost biblical figures, striding about like Old Testament prophets, insisting upon 'simple' values, and exhibiting a patriarchal sentiment for the 'eternal' Indian village. Their system was a highly efficient and rigidly controlled military government designed to impose, in the shortest possible time, the scaffolding of a civilized state. The utilitarian ideal was most apparent in the system of regular reports and collection of statistics, and the *animateur* of the system was not so much John Lawrence, who has received most of the praise, as Lord Dalhousie (governor-general 1848–56).

Dalhousie was an authoritarian reformer in the utilitarian mould, but he admitted no slavish adherence to abstract political theories. He was an active modernizer. He expanded the area of direct British rule. He considered the remaining native states to be anachronistic, and would have been delighted to annex them all. Primarily, however, Dalhousie was determined to transform India into a modern state. He created new, all-India departments to deal with civil engineering works, telegraphs, railways and the post office. Uniformity of management and unity of authority were his guiding principles —and the phrases themselves have the authentic utilitarian sound. But paradoxically, Dalhousie also encouraged the transformation of the legislative council into a sort of parliament, and advocated the appointment of Indian members to the council.

By the time the Charter Act came up for renewal in 1853, most opinion, both British and Indian, was opposed to Dalhousie's plans. The Act tinkered with the administration, but it was obvious that the Company's tenure was running out and that the day was not far distant when the Crown would take over the direct administration of India.

Despite the anticipated change in the relationship between Britain and India, which gave rise to some uncertainties, the general movement of reform associated with the name of Dalhousie continued to influence the existing system. The movement had the guarded approval of all who maintained an interest in India, whether they were theoreticians of government or businessmen anxious to enhance their profits. It represented, in effect, a new climate of optimism in England, where the industrial troubles of the 'Hungry Forties' were over and a new wave of prosperity had hit the manufacturing classes. Again, the ideals and hopes which had inspired the first reformers produced the heady vision of an anglicized India. Again, too, education appeared as the key to happiness and greater markets for British goods. Now, too, had come the great single tool of material progress—for India was about to enter the railway age. Charles Trevelyan, who had written in 1838 of the regenerating virtues of English schooling, hailed the railway as the means by which 'the whole machinery of society will be stimulated' and 'every other improvement whatever, both physical and moral' intensified.

The belief that Britain had a *mission civilisatrice* in India as well as active concern for the welfare of the people survived the trauma of the Mutiny of 1857. In fact, concern for the well-being of the 'patient, humble, silent millions', if anything, increased. But it did so as a consequence of the repudiation of the idea fundamental to the earlier era of reform, that of co-operation between the British and an emerging Indian middle class.

6

THE EXHAUSTED PURPOSE

After the débâcle of the Mutiny, the aim of the British in India was to impose a modern and efficient administration, operated by experts within the scaffolding of a codified law. The principles were to be English principles and *only* English principles. John Lawrence put the case in 1858 when he wrote: 'We have not been elected or placed in power by the people, but we are here through our moral superiority, by the force of circumstances, by the will of Providence. This alone constitutes our charter to govern India. In doing the best we can for the people, we are bound by our conscience, and not by theirs.' As a good paternalist, he believed in simple, personal rule. As viceroy (1864–9), he resisted the creation of an executive council for Bengal which had been removed from the governor-general's immediate authority in 1854. His opposition was based on the thesis that the best form of government emerged from a personal administration with a strong central authority. Dalhousie had already advocated the abolition of the governorships of Madras and Bombay in 1853. Lawrence reinforced this with his view that there was 'as strong a necessity as there possibly could be, for one central absolute authority in India, to which all other authorities in that country must entirely defer'.

There was, however, opposition in Britain to any form of centralization in India. There was, too, the fear that had been expressed at the end of the previous century by Edmund Burke that unchecked despotism would inevitably lead to corruption and oppression. In 1784, the government had set up a board of control in Britain, with a member of the British government at its head, to oversee the Company's rule. Even after 1858 —with the Company dead, and direct authority for the governing of India invested in a minister of the Crown—it was still thought necessary to hold on to some principle of control, some balance of authorities. To check the activities of the secretary of state for India, a Council of India was set up, consisting in the main of former directors and employees of the Company. The secretary of state was obliged to consult this council before sending instructions to India; in emergencies, however, he was empowered to act without it. Parliament also attempted to develop effective control over Indian affairs by requiring that an annual statement of finances and of moral and material progress should be submitted to the House of Commons.

Sir Charles Wood, who had been president of the board of control from 1853 to 1855, was secretary of state between 1859 and 1866. In this capacity he favoured decentralization in India. The provincial governments were permitted to retain their quasi-independent state *vis-à-vis* the government of India. The government of India itself was made entirely subordinate to the home government; at least, legally so.

All these assorted checks and balances did not permit any belief in the advisability—or even the possibility—of some form of representative institutions in India. The checks were regarded as a means of restraining concentration of power at the centre, not only because such concentration was considered morally indefensible but because it left too large a margin for error. One man's decision, if he had no guidance from the opinions of others, could lead to disastrous results in terms of human life. It was suggested, for example, that if the lieutenant-governor of Bengal had had an executive council to advise him, the Bengal administration would have been less unprepared for the terrible famine which broke out in Orissa in 1866; the decision not to act had been taken by the lieutenant-governor alone. The complexities of the modern state could not permit decision to rest in the hands of one man. It was a question of efficiency, no more.

Parliament also expected the legislative council to play an important role—though not in limiting despotism. Its function was to be a 'public' forum for discussing the acts of the government. In the Central Legislative Assembly, Dalhousie had seen the germ of a representative institution, but when the Indian Councils Act of 1861 was passed, any such possibility was explicitly denied. The new Act allowed for the nomination of 'non-official' Indians and Europeans to the legislative councils, but they were there to offer advice, not to represent any sector of popular opinion. The viceroy of the time, Lord Canning, who had been the last governor-general under Company rule, believed that Dalhousie had made a great mistake in implying that the central legislative council bore any resemblance to a parliament. Nevertheless, Canning was aware of the growing interest among educated Indians in the activities of government and believed that, in some way, it should be satisfied. Bartle Frere, an experienced British official, remarked that he himself knew

few things more striking than the change which has come over the Natives in this respect. Twenty years ago they were remarkable for their general indifference to all public questions which had no immediate local bearing. But this indifference has given place among the more intelligent classes to a feverish curiosity which has of late years frequently struck me as one of the most noteworthy changes in the general characteristics of Native society.

It was essential, Frere believed, that the government should have some way of knowing whether or not the laws it passed were sensible without having to wait for a rebellion to prove it.

There was to be no confirmation, however, of Dalhousie's premise that the Central Legislative Assembly might develop a representative character. Sir Charles Wood expressed the matter with some precision in the House of Commons in June 1861. 'You cannot possibly', he said, 'assemble at any one place in India persons who shall be the real representatives of the various classes of the Native population of that empire.'

The concept of Indian government enshrined in the Act of 1861 was one of despotism tempered, but not controlled, by discussion. As well as placing checks on personal authority, the Act did reflect certain political considerations. It was felt that some reward was necessary for those who had remained loyal to the British during the Mutiny. The first three Indians nominated to the central legislative council were therefore the Maharaja of Patiala, who had supplied a force to help the British; Raja Dinkar Rao Raghunath, *divan* (prime minister) of the Maharaja of Gwalior; and Raja Deo Narain Singh, another supporter of British rule. In fact, all Indians appointed to the council before the reforms of 1892 seem to have been awarded the honour in payment for their own or their fathers' support during the Mutiny.

The existence of legislative councils did not affect either the functioning of the government or what might be termed the philosophical preoccupations of some of its members. Ever since the first utilitarians, India had been treated as a kind of laboratory for political experiment. It did not cease to be so after the assumption of power by the Crown; the utilitarian tradition was long-lived, even though it needed reinterpretation in the circumstances of post-Mutiny India. The outstanding problem was not new. It was the same as the problem to which Cornwallis and Munro had given rival answers. Was the administration of India to be government by law, or government by personal discretion?

A new interpretation was supplied by Sir James Fitzjames Stephen, law member from 1869 until 1872. According to Stephen, the problem was how to reconcile the rule of law with the energy of the man on the spot. 'The question is between one kind of law and legal administration and another, not between government by law and government without law. The question, indeed, lies much more between different forms of administration than different forms of law.' A modern state, must, he argued, be an efficient and highly co-ordinated organization following precise rules and free from individual eccentricities. At the same time, the executive arm of the government should not be weakened by legal rigidity. 'The maintenance of the position of the District Officers is absolutely essential to the maintenance of British rule in India.' Stephen's solution was to leave the administration of criminal law with the executive, while allocating civil law to the judiciary. His reasons were not new: the man who ruled should be the man able to inflict punishment. 'In a few words, the administration of criminal justice is the indispensable condition of all government, and the means by which it is in the last resort carried on. But the District Officers are the local governors of the country; therefore, the District Officers ought to administer criminal justice.' Stephen was, in fact, convinced that a strong and vigorous government was perfectly compatible with the rule of law. 'The notion', he wrote, 'that there is an opposition in the nature of things between law and executive vigour, rests on a fundamental confusion of ideas and on traditions which are superannuated and ought to be forgotten.'

Stephen likened the administration of India to a highly disciplined army with well-defined instructions and efficient organization. He continued the work of law codification, relating much that had previously come under administrative orders to the structure of formal law. His attitude was purely practical, and he was little concerned with theories. He found the general structure of law and administration good, and contented himself with suggesting remedies for specific defects. What was really needed, he thought, was better training for officials. Whatever may have been the defects of Indian government, want of interest in the work done, want of vigilance in superintending the manner in which it was done, want of energy and enterprise in improving the manner of doing it, were not amongst them.

As law member, Stephen believed as strongly as his predecessors had done in the revolutionary effects of the rule of law. Indeed, he was convinced that the destruction of the Indian village community by means of English concepts of property rights and the rule of English law was an example of progress.

> The fact that the institutions of a village community throw light on the institutions of modern Europe, and the fact that village communities had altered but little for many centuries, prove only that society in India has remained for a great number of centuries in a stagnant condition, unfavourable to the growth of wealth, intelligence, political experience, and the moral and intellectual changes which are implied in these processes. The condition of India for centuries past shows what the village communities are really worth. Nothing that deserves the name of a political institution at all can be ruder or less satisfactory than its results. They are, in fact, a crude form of socialism, paralysing the growth of individual energy and all its consequences. The continuation of such a state of society is radically inconsistent with the fundamental principles of our rule both in theory and in practice.

Stephen also considered that there was no need to interfere in personal law relating to Hindus and Muslims. The actions of modern government would, in themselves, create such changes as were needed.

There was nothing paternalistic about Stephen's views. The break-up of village communities and the transfer of land to money-lenders appeared to him a necessary part of the pains of progress. But neither did he contemplate associating the

Indian middle classes with the administration. In this, his views made a distinct break with the liberalism of the 1830s, which had envisaged not only co-operation between the races but even ultimate self-government for India. Both Stephen and John Strachey—who became a member of the viceroy's executive council in 1868 and finance member in 1876—accepted the fact that, for simple economic reasons, educated Indians should be given government appointments and even consulted on legislative questions. But both were convinced, as Strachey was to put it, that it would be the beginning of the end for the Empire if major executive powers were entrusted

to the hands of Natives, on the assumption that they will always be faithful and strong supporters of our government. In this there is nothing offensive or disparaging to the Natives of India. It simply means that we are foreigners, and that, not only in our own interests, but because it is our highest duty towards India itself, we intend to maintain our dominion. We cannot foresee the time in which the cessation of our rule would not be the signal for universal anarchy and ruin, and it is clear that the only hope for India is the long continuance of the benevolent but strong government of Englishmen. Let us give to the Natives the largest possible share in the administration . . . But let there be no hypocrisy about our intention to keep in the hands of our own people those executive posts—and there are not very many of them—on which, and in our military and political power, our actual hold of the country depends. Our Governors of provinces, the chief officers of our army, our magistrates of districts and their principal executive subordinates ought to be Englishmen under all circumstances that we can now foresee.

This rejection of any major co-operation from the various sectors of Indian society soon came under attack in both India and Britain. Faced with a growing sense of Indian nationalism, a trade recession, famine, and agrarian rioting in the 1870s, Lord Lytton (viceroy 1876–80) concluded that it was foolish for the government not to seek support from at least one level of Indian society. As a Conservative, he favoured the claims of the Indian aristocracy. In May 1877, he wrote:

I am convinced that the fundamental mistake of able and experienced Indian officials is a belief that we can hold India securely by what they call good government; that is to say, by improving the condition of the peasant, strictly administering justice, spending immense sums on irrigation works, etc. Politically speaking, the Indian peasantry is an inert mass. If it ever moves at all, it will move in obedience, not to its British benefactors, but to its native chiefs and princes, however tyrannical they may be. The only political representatives of native opinion are the Baboos, whom we have educated to write semi-seditious articles in the native Press, and who really represent nothing but the social anomaly of their own position . . . To secure completely, and efficiently utilise, the Indian aristocracy is, I am convinced, the most important problem now before us.

Although the British prime minister, Disraeli, responded in the same year by proclaiming Queen Victoria as Empress of India, it made no difference to the character of the Indian administration. In fact, the government made it even more difficult for Indians to become candidates for the Indian Civil Service by reducing the examination age from twenty-one to nineteen. Nevertheless, it claimed to agree with Lytton when he attached 'great importance to the obvious political expediency of endeavouring to strengthen our administration by attracting to it that class of Natives whose social position or connections give to them a commanding influence over their countrymen'. A special branch, known as the Statutory Civil

Service, was formed in 1879 in which prominent Indians could be employed. The service was, however, abolished on the recommendation of the Indian Public Service Commission of 1886–7 and replaced in 1892 by new cadres of the provincial and subordinate Civil Service, reserved for Indians.

Between the years 1876 and 1880, the Liberal party—in opposition in Britain—indulged in a crusade against the government's India policy, attacking the bill which made Queen Victoria Empress of India as well as the restrictive legislation passed by the government of India in 1878 against native-language newspapers. In an article published in 1877, the Liberal leader, William Ewart Gladstone, argued that, morally, it was necessary that India should be governed for the good of Indians. Furthermore, he said, the British had actually created an Indian middle class, and they owed it to that class to govern in just such a manner.

> The question who shall have supreme rule in India is, by the laws of right, an Indian question; and those laws of right are from day to day growing into laws of fact. Our title to be there depends upon a first condition, that our being there is profitable to the Indian nation; and on a second condition, that we can make them see and understand it to be profitable ... It is high time that [these truths] pass from the chill elevation of political philosophy into the warmth of contact with daily life; that they take their place in the working rules, and that they limit the daily practice, of the agents of our power ... for unless they do, we shall not be prepared to meet an inevitable future, we shall not be able to confront the growth of the Indian mind under the very active processes of education which we have ourselves introduced.

The Liberals' opportunity came with their success in the elections of 1880, and during the viceroyalty of Lord Ripon (1880–4) a number of reforms took place—against considerable opposition from some quarters in India. The restrictive Press Act was repealed and steps were taken to breathe at least some life into organs of local self-government.

An attempt had been made during the viceroyalty of Lord Mayo (1869–72) to establish working municipal institutions. Mayo wrote:

> We must gradually associate with ourselves in the Government of this country more of the native element. We have neglected this too much ... I believe that we shall find the best assistance from natives in our administration, not by competitive examination or the sudden elevation of ill educated and incapable men, but by quietly entrusting as many as we can with local responsibility, and instructing them in the management of their own district affairs.

The experiment had not been successful.

When Ripon tried to give the municipal councils real power and initiative, he was resisted both by British officials and by the majority of the non-official British community. The opposition, complained Ripon, came from the type of man 'who regards India and her inhabitants as made for his advantage and for that alone, who never looks upon himself in any other light than that of a conqueror, and upon the natives as otherwise than as "subject races" '. In Britain, too, there was considerable opposition to Ripon's general policies. Fitzjames Stephen, in a letter to *The Times* on 1 March 1883, attacked them on the grounds that Ripon and the government intended to shift 'the first foundations on which the British Government of India rests'.

In fact, Gladstone's policies—not only in India—were producing a split amongst Liberals and alienating particularly those intellectuals who had seen Liberalism as the servant of great political causes and the symbol of a dynamic and positive individualism. All this appeared menaced by the rise of democracy. It was this and Gladstone's apparent willingness to dismantle the Empire—the Irish Home Rule Bill seemed the first step—which put the great experiment of India in peril. Gladstone's actions and attitudes stimulated a variety of responses, not only defence of the 'ideology' of Indian government, but new statements of imperial purpose and responsibility.

Stephen, in his writings, had postulated the special role of the law. It was, he said, 'the gospel of the English . . . and a compulsory gospel which admits of no dissent and no disobedience'. The operation of the law depended on the State's coercive powers, which should not be eroded by any extension of representative institutions. The situation was, he suggested, bad enough in Britain now that the franchise was being extended. In India, if the authority of the government were once materially relaxed, 'if the essential character of the enterprise is misunderstood and the delusion that it can be carried out by assemblies representing the opinions of the natives is admitted, nothing but failure, anarchy, and ruin can be the result.'

Reverence for the law implied a responsibility to uphold it and a duty to expand its beneficent rule. The early Christian reformers in India had been conscious of the immanence of God and of the need to bring the heathen into his fold. Once inside, they believed, happiness was assured. This belief had been so strong that it had even distorted the application of the essentially non-religious ideas of the utilitarians. By Stephen's time, however, it was becoming fashionable to dispute the existence of God and the supernatural world, and that fear of divine retribution which had lain behind the actions of the early reformers had lost its force. Substitutes had to be found which would inspire the new imperialism with a zeal similar to that which had formerly drawn its strength from Christianity.

Such substitutes already existed within the British intellectual tradition. Carlyle had fiercely defended the proposition that might was right and that the principal factor in man's religion was man's work. Other philosophers also propounded the new gospel in which worship was replaced by 'service' and God by 'country'. In this way, all the enthusiasm of religion was transferred to purely secular objects. The gospel of the new religion of patriotism was the gospel of duty, of work done without fear of criticism or expectation of gratitude. Its virtues were self-denial, law, order and obedience.

The doctrines of the new religion of empire were military doctrines and were based upon the use of force, authority and direction. In Stephen's view, there was no widespread desire in India for representative institutions; if there had been, it probably could not have been resisted. But educated Indians were the tiniest of minorities, interested only in their own advantage and not in that of the mass of India's people.

Such an authoritarian view did not go unchallenged. There were those who thought that the best way to rule a dependent empire was to do so indirectly, by using indigenous institutions and manipulating the puppets of a native ruling class. This was the attitude favoured by Cromer in Egypt and other imperialists in Malaya and Nigeria. Cromer had acquired his colonial experience in India, as had Sir Alfred Lyall, who was the spokesman for many theorists of indirect rule. These men, and others who thought as they did, believed just as wholeheartedly as Stephen and Strachey in the moral approach to political power, and its exercise. But they differed by refusing to accept force and military strength as the basis of that power. Nor did they believe in what has come to be called the Westernization of alien societies by imposing sophisticated political institutions which had no traditional roots. Lyall, for example, maintained that the effect of Western civilization on India was to dissolve the bonds of Indian society without putting anything in their place. Concentration of power in the hands of the British, who were indifferent to the traditional demands and pressures of Indian society, was producing, said Lyall, 'that condition of

over-centralized isolation with shallow foundations and inadequate support, which renders an empire as top-heavy as an
over-built tower'. Lyall and Cromer were both convinced that
there had to be some compromise between the 'civilizing' acts
of the British and the feelings of the people, and that the British
must therefore develop some genuine respect for the traditional beliefs and institutions of their subjects. If this were not
forthcoming, discontent would surely polarize and lead to an
attack upon the alien rulers as the only remaining symbol of
authority. According to Lyall and others, legitimate scope for
expression should be given to India's princes and educated
classes.

On the surface, the theorists of indirect rule appeared to be
advocating a policy which was designed to permit competing
elements to cancel each other out. It was certainly not, however, conceived for that purpose.

But Lyall did propose a quieter administration and the
abandonment of aggressive legislation. In fact, after 1885,
there developed a period of inertia in Indian administration.

The growth of Indian nationalism after the founding of the
Indian National Congress in 1885 brought pressure on the
government of India to reform the councils. The government's
own feeling was that some reform was not only necessary but
sensible, and that if something were not done Britain would, in
the words of the viceroy, Lord Dufferin, 'soon have something
like a Home Rule organization established in India, on Irish
lines, and under the patronage of Irish and Radical Members
of [the British] Parliament'.

In 1892 a new Councils Act was passed by the Conservative
government in Britain, with the full support of the Liberal
opposition. It was intended as a sop to nationalist demands.
Under the new Act, the provincial councils—though not the
viceroy's central council—were to be permitted to discuss
questions relating to administration and the budget, and the
majority of non-official seats were to be filled on the 'recom-

mendation' of such groups as municipalities, chambers of commerce and religious communities. This amounted in practice to a system of elections. The Act was a triumph of practical politics. Nothing essential had been given away, but some concessions had been seen to have been made. The co-operation between Conservatives and Liberals in the passing of the Act showed that the Liberals were accepting what might be called the necessities of empire—the fact that the possession of overseas dominions might dictate policy rather than respond to abstract theories.

All this activity, however, did not touch the actual administration of India. Even the matter of local self-government lay in an area almost insulated from the realities of everyday life. The trend of administration towards simple efficiency and more Western-type institutions was no more than a trend. Stephen might conceive the Indian State as a sort of leviathan, but it was nothing of the sort. Adaptations of practice were constantly taking place, and on grounds other than economy—though economy did limit the size of the administration. In tribal areas, a much simpler system operated, using indigenous institutions. The authoritarian spirit certainly existed in the administration, but as an ideal rather than a reality. By the time the last exponent of dynamic purpose arrived in India in the person of Lord Curzon (viceroy, 1898–1905), the administration had become ponderous, like an elephant—'very stately, very powerful, with a high standard of intelligence, but with a regal slowness in its gait'.

Curzon sought to bring to India a new sense of purpose or, rather, a sense of the old purpose writ large and expressed in the vocabulary of the new century. Like his mentors, Stephen and Strachey, he was convinced that India was the keystone in the arch of British power. He was, in fact, the epitome of intellectual imperialism. His aim was to overhaul the machine so that it might push India into the modern world. He believed in looking to the future. It was, he claimed, the fundamental

duty of his administration 'everywhere to look ahead; to scruti-
nize not merely the passing requirements of the hour, but the
abiding needs of the country; and to build not for the present
but for the future.' With this as the firm foundation of his
policy, he tried to restore to British rule in India the creative
energy of the first era of reform; he tried, too, to purge it of that
contempt for even the best of Indian civilization and culture,
which had corroded and helped to destroy the reformist
purpose. Curzon believed that the destiny of the Indian people
had been entrusted by Providence to the British. This was the
lesson of the past, and a lesson which he believed was being
confirmed by the present.

The British had created—and how else but with the assistance of Providence?—the greatest empire the world had ever
seen. They had been granted the secret of the machine, the
power with which to dominate not only men, but the forces of
nature as well. It is difficult for us today, with our different view
of the historical process, to accept Curzon's idea of history as
anything other than humbug, a cynical *realpolitik* explained as
the work of God's invisible hand. But in the nineteenth and
early twentieth centuries, awed by the majesty, by the very
physical extent of their dominions, it was hardly surprising that
the British should turn to divine interpretations. The God
whose hand they saw in all their deeds was, of course, a very
British God, imbued with British virtues, speaking—as it
were—their own language. Formal Christianity may have
played little part in the religion of the imperialists, but they an-
thropomorphized a god who embodied the ideal of their empire.

This view was peculiarly sophisticated—and eminently
satisfying. It raised the British Empire from a mere conquest
and a continuing tyranny to the status of a dynamic crusade,
pledged to the greatest happiness for the greatest number. Its
motivating force was duty, and its purpose to construct the
promised land. At a banquet in February 1903, Curzon said:

If I thought it were all for nothing, and that you and I, Englishmen, Scotchmen and Irishmen in this country, were simply writing inscriptions on the sand to be washed out by the next tide; if I felt that we were not working here for the good of India in obedience to a higher law and a nobler aim, then I would see the link that holds India and England together severed without a sigh. But it is because I believe in the future of this country and the capacity of our own race to guide it to goals that it has never hitherto attained, that I keep courage and press forward.

With such a creed, Curzon could admit no meaningful place for Indians themselves except as recipients of British beneficence. Indian intellectuals, Indian nationalists who claimed the right to lead the masses, had to be brushed aside as grit in the great machine. The Indian princes had to be acknowledged; their subjects could not be denied the benefits of English rule merely because archaic treaties gave the princes at least some measure of independence. But the peasants were the main target of reform; from improvement to their condition would come the justification of British rule. 'While I have sought', Curzon declared in his farewell speech in Bombay, 'to understand the needs and to espouse the interests of each [of India's various races and creeds]—my eye has always rested on a larger canvas crowded with untold numbers, the real people of India.'

The difference between Curzon and Dalhousie, the last great reforming governor-general among Curzon's predecessors, was not merely a half century of conservatism. The philosophers and theorists whose executive arm Dalhousie was, had believed that India could be changed into a simulacrum of the West by opening her doors and allowing English education, English morals and English conceptions of justice to flood in. Curzon, observing at the end of the nineteenth century the effects of the invasion of Western liberal ideas, felt something of the disintegration it was bringing about. He saw that a minority of Indians had derived from English education a political vocabulary with which they could question and dispute British rule, but that their learning contributed nothing to help the mass of the people. He sought, by diverting a new generation of Indians into technical education, to convert them from talkers into doers. The ideal of early reformers had been to make Indians into liberal Englishmen; Curzon wanted to make them into scientists and technicians. He believed that, if he managed to inspire them with the same enthusiasm as impelled the younger generation in Britain, they could transform India.

Curzon's was a vision of startling modernity, and one which today underlies the whole philosophy of economic planning in the underdeveloped countries of the world. In this sense, he came to India too soon, but in the political sense he had arrived too late. It was no longer possible to ignore the demands of educated Indians or those of revivalist nationalism.

When Curzon left India in 1905—as the result of a clash with the government in London fundamentally concerned with civil control of the armed forces in India—the purpose which he had sought to revitalize and restate was really exhausted, the high noon of empire past. But the captains and the kings had not yet departed, had neither booked their passages nor even begun to pack their bags. The British appeared, behind the glorious façade of pomp and circumstance which on the whole delighted both British and Indians, as firmly entrenched as ever. But the glitter of power, the magnificence of the uniforms, hid the weakness—and fragility—of the Raj.

Until 1909, the British government and the Indian services were agreed on at least one thing—that the best form of government for India was despotism. The men who ruled India saw themselves in one sense as *Indian* rulers, carrying on a traditional form of government which had operated in India before the British conquered it. But this despotism was transformed by the British ideas of responsibility and 'fair play'; the administrators saw it not as an exploitive despotism but as a creative one. Very few of them believed that democratic institutions could work in India and they feared that the British parliament, desperately ignorant as its members were about India, would try to force such institutions on the country. Their attitude was based partly on administrative experience and partly on a fear that any weakening of British authority—which the involvement of Indians in a government would certainly mean—might lead to disorder. The British knew that they had the strength to suppress isolated rioting but not, perhaps, a well-organized revolt. The memory of 1857 was never too far away from the minds of the British in India.

The effect of material progress in India, of railways, cheap postal services, and of the spread of English as the language for the whole of India, began to produce a new sense of Indian unity. For the first time in India's history, a man of the south could feel he had something in common with the man of the north, the east and the west. The number of British administrators was never more than 3,000 or 4,000, and below them they had a vast force of Indian subordinates. The army, too, was predominantly Indian. Thus, as material progress spread in India, so did the possibilities of successful revolt.

The district officer, carrying out his duties with benevolent despotism, began to see his authority diminished by various quasi-democratic boards and councils. Partisan attitudes arose. The peasant, who had looked to the district officer for impartiality, had done so precisely because he was not an Indian and because there were other Englishmen higher up to whom the peasant could appeal if the district officer failed him. But as changes took place, he observed that the district officer was being subjected to other pressures; the new district boards might include the brother of the peasant's landlord or the second cousin of the money-lender. It seemed to the peasant that such board members as these, and the sectional interests they represented, would make a fair hearing of his own case impossible. The district officer's impartiality appeared diminished, and he could probably be bypassed by influential men. Such a state of affairs could only lead to dissatisfaction, to disaffection and unease. As the government of India at its real level, the district, was based not on a display of power but on the consent of respect, administration would not function if that respect was eroded.

This was what the rulers of India feared and they did not see how the situation could be avoided if the British parliament insisted on granting representative institutions. As long as such institutions were confined to local government, the district officer could rely on receiving support from his own kind in the government in the province and even from the centre; but, as reform spread to these places too, he became sadly aware that his days were numbered. He began to have fears about his future, his pension rights, the justifiable rewards of good and honest service. Young men, who had once been anxious for the opportunity of ruling India, began to think of other and safer careers. Edward Thompson, in one of his unjustly neglected novels of the twenties and thirties of this century, makes one of his characters say of the British in India: 'We neither govern nor misgovern. We're just hanging on, hoping that the Last Trump will sound "Time!" and save us from the bother of making a decision.' Day-to-day administration went on but the British came to feel themselves caretakers rather than owners, concerned only with keeping the structure in repair and unwilling to make improvements or alterations.

This journey from heroism to stoicism is encapsulated in a simple change of words in an inscription on the base of a statue to John Lawrence in Lahore. On its first erection in the 1870s, the bronze likeness, which brandished a pen in one hand and a sword in the other, was supported on a plinth bearing the rousing words: *I have offered you the alternative—the Pen or the Sword.* During the years of political unrest, these two symbols were often broken and, as often, replaced. But in the 1920s, restoration revealed that the inscription now read: *I have served you with both Pen and Sword*!

The statement of defiant will had been superseded by the melancholy justification of the epitaph.

7

PERCEPTIONS OF INDIA

Empires are more than territory, occupied space, geopolitical entities. They exist also in the minds, not only of those who possess them, but of those who envy them their possession. For outsiders, the image of a British Empire, on which the sun never set, created and sustained not only the reality but the illusion of power. For those inside, for the men who actually administered the Empire, the image in the mind was essential both for efficiency and for psychic health. How these men perceived not only themselves and their civilization, but also the peoples they ruled and *their* civilization was as important to the maintenance and security of the Empire as armed force. More so, for such perceptions added to that force the strengths of reason, purpose and destiny.

For the first fifty years of their rule in India, the British never felt wholly secure or even convinced of the permanence of their dominion. They were often critical of what they saw around them, but they were careful not to allow their feelings to influence their actions in case it aroused opposition which they might not be in a position to resist. At the same time, they had some respect for Indian culture or at least certain aspects of it. In the eighteenth century there was considerable social inter-course between the British and the Muslim aristocracies. Many British officials spoke and read Persian, the literary language. Some of them regarded themselves as Indian rulers. On one level, those British in India who had no intellectual interests enjoyed the superficial luxuries of Indian aristocratic life. English women, because they were few in a masculine society, generally accepted the men's opinion. They, too, enjoyed the luxuries. They were not in the least worried at attending balls and dinners given by Indians, even though Indian women were not present.

Towards the end of the century, however, the British were becoming conscious of a sense of racial superiority. The easy social relations they had had with Indians began to decline, though at first only in Calcutta. In other parts of India, where English society was numerically small and fashionable attitudes slow to arrive, the old relations with Indians continued.

The change in the social attitude began with the arrival of Lord Cornwallis in 1786. His purpose was to reform the administration, to clean up corruption and nepotism amongst the British. He succeeded. But in his desire to create a body of honest officials, he also excluded Indians from the higher posts of government. Cornwallis was convinced that every 'native of Hindustan' was corrupt. Unlike his predecessor, Warren Hastings, he had no intellectual interests to bridge the gap between himself and the Indian aristocracy. He replaced native judges with English judges. He abandoned, almost entirely, the traditional etiquette of diplomatic relations. Cornwallis succeeded in forcing the old Indian governing classes into isolation, leaving behind them only the Indian servant, the clerk, the merchant and the banker as representatives of India and Indian culture.

Not unnaturally, the remainder of the British community took its lead from senior officials and, in particular, the governor-general. As they withdrew from contact, so did lesser beings. By 1810, a visitor to Calcutta was able to report that 'every Briton appears to pride himself on being outrageously a John Bull'.

The government's attitude was strengthened and expanded by Lord Wellesley who, arriving in India in 1798, brought with him a profound sense of racial arrogance. He had come to enlarge Britain's dominions—against the wishes of his nominal masters, the directors of the East India Company—and imperialism needs the backing of pride, the consciousness of superiority. Wellesley had nothing but contempt for Indians.

There were other factors which contributed to the growing estrangement between Indians and the British. One of these was the growing number of women in the British settlements. They tended to bring with them the English prejudices of their time. Their attitude, generally speaking, was Christian, and narrowly so. They brought, too, a new sense of family life, and their arrival resulted in the expulsion of native mistresses who had at least injected something of India into the world of the British. The women had little to occupy their minds. Their life was a tedious social round. But they did have gossip. In a novel describing life in the 1840s, one character is made to remark:

'In other parts of the world they talk about things, here they talk about people . . .'

'But what,' said Peregrine, 'do the people find to say about one another?'

'Oh!' returned Miss Poggleton; 'the veriest trifles in the world. Nothing is so insignificant as the staple of Calcutta conversation. What Mr. This said to Miss That, and what Miss That did to Mr. This; and then all the interminable gossip about marriages and no-marriages, and will-be-marriages and ought-to-be-marriages, and gentlemen's attention and ladies' flirtings, dress reunions, and the last big dinners—'

'Pictures, taste, Shakespeare, and the musical glasses,' suggested Peregrine, with a smile.

'Oh! dear no, nothing half as good as that,' returned Julia Poggleton; 'the only Shakespeare known in Calcutta is a high civilian of that name.'

The women were not interested in Indians, only in the in-efficiencies of their servants. They wanted to create for themselves and their menfolk an island in the vast sea of India—and to a large extent they were successful.

Another factor in the estrangement was the influence of Christian missionaries who, though they mixed freely with Indians, had nothing but horror for their religion and frequently said so in the most violent terms. Their criticisms had great effect on the British in India, convincing them that it would hardly be worth while to make an attempt at any close relationship with such a barbarous people.

But the principal contribution to racial attitudes came from the expansion of British society in India. Gradually, it became large enough to take on a life and a character of its own. It was no longer necessary for a small number of Englishmen to accept what India had to offer for their pleasure. English society in the principal towns and stations was now able to supply all that was needed, the support and understanding of fellow-countrymen, and a simulated England in which English life might be enjoyed. As the number of British men and women increased, they were able to construct a fortress into which to retire after the unavoidable engagements with the natives—in business, in the law, or in government. It also gave them something to defend and to justify.

Breaches were occasionally made in the barriers that were being erected between the British and the Indians, but their effect was largely nullified by that feeling of superiority which was at once self-defence and an inspiration for social reform. The 'revelations' concerning widow-burning, female infanticide, and the Thugs, which led to the major reforms of Lord William Bentinck, intensified the British community's distaste for Indians and their way of life. After 1820, the evangelical Christianity of many of the Company's officers led them to see evil in almost everything Indian.

This attitude was not shared by everyone in India, though even in the case of those who showed most respect for Indians and their institutions there was a basic element of contempt.

But the individuals who did manage to bridge the gulf between themselves and Indians were exceptions. As British rule spread across India and Englishmen came out from Britain in increasing numbers to administer the new territories, such attempts were regarded as more and more eccentric, un-English and generally to be condemned. There were undertones of condescension even among those officials who advocated reform, although they believed they were doing the right thing for India as well as for Britain.

As they acquired a sense of purpose, the British in India began to acquire a sense of duty. They had always felt themselves to be exiles, a feeling reinforced by the rigours of the Indian climate. The author of the novel quoted before said; 'The great world is full of changes, but the Calcutta world is far more changeable than any of the lesser ones it contains in its vast cycle. Society, in these parts, is a sort of ever-moving procession, and the same characters are seldom to be seen on the stage many months together.' What he meant was that the threat of an early grave hung over everyone. The atmosphere in which the land itself was an enemy certainly affected the judgement of many. It reinforced their dislike of India and explained, too, the occasional outbursts of hysteria among the British population.

By the 1850s, the British in India had virtually institutionalized their contempt for things Indian and successfully resisted reforms which they believed would lower their standing 'in the eyes of the natives'. They were able to resist, successfully, the government's attempt to equalize the application of the law. In 1837, the government passed what was known as the 'Black Act', designed to make British residents outside Calcutta subject to the jurisdiction of the Company's courts, in which Indian judges might preside. British residents sent a petition to parliament, and the Act was not enforced. All the British in India, official and non-official alike, used the same standards of judgement—those of their own country and their own culture. They discovered that practically everything Indian fell short of those standards, in business, in government and in religion. A minority continued to suggest that something valuable could be learned from Indian experience, something that might help decide how best to run the country. But it was always a minority. After about 1830, though changes developed in the standards of judgement, both the changes and the standards were always British.

The British community was taken by surprise in 1857 when the Bengal army began its rebellion. The British had assumed that all was quiet, that the reforming and progressive actions of government had spread only gratitude and affection. When reports came in of the massacre of British soldiers and their wives and children, they were horrified and called loudly for revenge. All elements gave way to hatred, but racial antagonism was strongest amongst the non-official merchant community and the planters. Although, when the Mutiny ended, the government was prepared to pursue a policy of conciliation, many of the British were not and the memory of the Mutiny remained as a constant reminder that it was unwise to trust the natives. It was a not unnatural reaction to the times when a trusted servant or a regimental soldier had suddenly changed, apparently without reason, into a murderer. In spite of the fact that many British came to realize, after the hot flush of the Mutiny had died down, that they and their government were not entirely blameless, the distrust never wholly disappeared.

After 1858, the numbers of the British, both official and non-official, increased steadily over the years. 'Anglo-Indian' society had its stratifications and was large enough to contain most of the activities of the British in India. Officials and soldiers were compelled—particularly outside the large towns —to have contact with Indians, but it was almost entirely *official* contact. Social relations were extremely rare, and the civil servant who was interested in Indian culture even rarer. The British became completely what they were already becoming in the last twenty years of Company rule—'a separate caste, with several sub-castes, strictly preserving the usual characteristics of endogamy, commensality, and mutual control by members'.

Social distance was ensured and reinforced by physical separation. The British official elite lived in carefully planned 'civil stations', with spacious houses surrounded by large gardens, the roads, wide and straight, in strong contrast to the 'native' city, with its narrow, congested streets and dirty alleys. When they could, the British got away altogether from the India of the plains, with its deadly heat and rampant disease, and fled to the cool hills, thus adding height to distance. In the foothills of the Himalayas, and in other high places, the British constructed simulacra of 'Home'. There the afternoons, as a poetic viceroy put it, could be 'rainy and the road muddy, but such beautiful *English* rain, such delicious *English* mud'.

There was nothing particularly reprehensible in the desire for the company of one's own race, in hill stations that added a touch of environmental illusion, or in the Club which offered the refuge of cultural exclusivity, however trivial. The danger lay in a not uncommon reversal of reality, in which the make-believe of the hill station and the racial togetherness of the Club became more real than the world outside. Such refuges became fortresses, stuffed with psychological weaponry, to use against the *threat* of India.

That threat was perceived on several levels. The most obvious was that of the middle-class, Western-educated Indian, asking for at least some role in the decision-making process. That could be handled best by a simple denial on the grounds that such Indians were in fact *deraciné*, not Indians at all. The best weapon against them was a rather heavy humour. The butt was usually the *babu* (a rather disparaging word for a clerk) and, in particular, the Bengali *babu*, as it was in Bengal that the awful effects of Western education had first manifested themselves. One humorist wrote in 1879:

When I was in Lhasa the Dalai Lama told me that a virtuous cow-hippopotamus by metempsychosis might, under un-favourable circumstances, become an undergraduate of the Calcutta University, and that, when patent-leather shoes and English supervened; the thing was a Baboo . . . The true Baboo is full of words and phrases—full of inappropriate words and phrases lying about like dead men on a battlefield, in heaps to be carted away promiscuously, without reference to kith or kin.

But still, behind the comedy, lurked a fear. 'When they wax fat with new religions, music, painting, Comedie Anglaise, scientific discoveries, they may kick with those well-developed legs of theirs, until we shall have to think they are something more than a joke, more than a mere *lusus naturae*, more than a caricature moulded in a moment of wanton playfulness.'

Laughter among friends and equals was less reassuring as a weapon against the other, perhaps the real, India, of the 'native' city, mysterious, alien—and seductive. There is always an element of attraction in the disordered and the anarchic, even if it is only the desire to impose order. Unfortunately, the British to a large extent were denied access to the 'real' India. They could observe the life of its streets, but not the lives lived out behind the walls of the houses. In the streets they saw dirt and—like such modern critics of our own times as V. S. Naipaul—they gagged at the smell of excrement. One of the main arguments against Indians running their own affairs was that they had no sense of the importance of sanitation. This lack of concern was symbolic, not only of the cultural gap between British and Indian, but also of the need of an in-efficient and weak-willed people for continuing dependence. The cloacal obsession of the British in India—an eminently sensible one in the context of endemic disease—became a metaphor of both racial superiority and paternalistic concern.

For the British, dirt had many concomitants. Ignorance and

superstition they saw in the gaudy religion of popular Hindu-ism, and were repelled and fascinated by it. 'The Mysterious East' has always been more than a travel writer's cliché. The 'dark' side of Indian life was as attractive to the Westerner in the 1960s as it was a century earlier, and for at least some of the same reasons, the most important of which is the element of *control*. The young Europeans and Americans who flocked to India in the 1960s did so in the hope that somewhere in Hindu belief and practice there was a secret method with which they might control their environment, a *magical* solution to what they judged to be the problems of advanced capitalist societies. The British in India knew, if only in their unconscious, that their power was essentially insubstantial. A former civil servant, looking back from the second decade of the twentieth century, wrote:

> Our life in India, our very hard work, more or less, rests on illusion. I had the illusion wherever I was that I was infallible and invulnerable in my dealing with Indians. How else could I have dealt with angry mobs, with cholera stricken masses, and with processions of religious fanatics? It was not conceit . . . it was not the prestige of the British Raj, but it was the illusion which is in the very air of India. They [Indians] expressed something of the idea when they called us the 'Heaven born', and the idea is really make-believe—mutual make-believe. They, the millions, made us believe we had a divine mission. We made them believe they were right . . . They had a vague conception of the Raj, which they looked on as a power, omnipotent, all-pervading, benevolent for the most part, but capricious, a deity of many shapes and many moods.

This 'imperial' magic of the rulers was only in part confrontational. In essence it was dynamically dependent on the magical and superstitious beliefs of the ruled. To the latter, the

British attitude was ambivalent, especially so when the other concomitants of dirt—lust and vice—were added to those of ignorance and superstition. The British found the overt sexual symbolism of Hindu worship both intriguing and repellent. Strangely enough, it was not the obvious phallicism of the god Siva (the worship of the ubiquitous *lingam*, a stylized though usually unmistakable penis, could hardly be ignored) but the destructive female sexuality of the goddess Kali that produced a *frisson* of fear and excitement. The British believed that it was the female in Indian society who not only emasculated their own kind, but threatened to castrate the Briton.

The British image of the Indian woman and the pervading sexuality of Indian society owed a great deal to lurid 'descriptions' of the zenana, the women's quarters, where behind doors always closed to the British male, a debilitating licentiousness was believed to reign. To counteract these intriguing pictures, and to discourage members of the ruling elite from in any way sampling their delights, the stereotype of the castrating Indian female was countered by the stereotype of the chaste, pure and above all respectable, Englishwoman. 'Anglo-Indian' literature, novels and memoirs, lingered over descriptions of the horrors of Indian life and the implied threat to the purity of English womanhood.

The stereotype of Indian sexuality was used to reinforce the need for social distance between the rulers and the ruled. The British could allow themselves an *interest*, like that of the social anthropologist, in the 'dark' side of Indian life, but they kept reminding themselves of their own superior magic. A young civil servant recalling the effect of observing life in Benares, the most holy city of Hindu India, at the turn of the century, noted: 'It was my first contact with the mysticism of the East, and superficial though it was, it fascinated me. It was perhaps as well that my brother, who had to deal with the problems of the famous pilgrim city, was there to draw my attentions to the *drains, the fountains and the police stations.*'

[109]

It was perhaps the fear of being seduced by the highly charged female sensuality the British associated with the plains and cities of India that was the most important factor in the idealization of the Frontier. Some Britons saw the north-west frontier of India in the same terms as Lord Curzon, who drew a parallel between the character-building nature of the American frontier experience 'and a corresponding discipline for the men of our stock . . . on the outskirts of Empire, where the machine is relatively impotent and the individual is strong'. On the Frontier a male society faced a male society. The Pathan tribesmen of the Indian borderlands were viewed with an admittedly qualified admiration—they were condemned for their cunning, treachery and violence, but praised for being as brave as lions and as wild as cats: 'noble savages' comparing favourably with the weak and degenerate plainsman. Even the allegedly pervasive 'vice' of homosexuality among the tribesmen—'a woman for business, a boy for pleasure'—though condemned, also fascinated because of its association with daring and reckless courage. There is, of course, a frequent tendency in the development of stereotypes to attribute to the other groups the characteristic most feared in one's own. At least the tribesman's apparent sexual preference offered no threat to English womanhood.

The British could hardly disguise the fact that at one time their relationships with Indian women could not have been more intimate. By the end of the nineteenth century, Eurasians numbered more than 80,000—half the European population. In the seventeenth century, the East India Company had encouraged the growth of an Eurasian community and not merely on the principle enshrined in the 'proverb' that 'Necessity is the Mother of Invention, and Father of the Eurasian.' A half-caste community would, it was believed, naturally identify with its fathers' race, and form what was in effect a permanent garrison in India. Army officers and civil servants had children by Indian wives and mistresses, and, for most of the eighteenth century, responsible positions in the army and the Civil Service were open to them. By the end of the century, however, Eurasians were excluded from positions in the Company's civil, military and marine services. Such positions were to be reserved for full-blooded Englishmen.

When a dominant group creates stereotypes, it does so by ignoring any fact that tends to undermine or invalidate those stereotypes. Eurasians were condemned for displaying the vices of both races, that 'Borderline where the last drop of White blood ends and the full tide of Black sets in', where 'the White shows in spurts of fierce, childish pride . . . the Black in . . . half-heathenish customs and strange unaccountable impulses to crime.' It was claimed that Eurasians could not make good army officers because Indian soldiers would despise them. That in the past there had been many highly successful Eurasian officers both in the East India Company's forces and in those of the Indian princes, was ignored. It was further maintained that Eurasians could not be competent medical officers because English ladies would be unwilling to consult them, despite substantial evidence to the contrary.

All the stereotypes in which the British encapsulated their perceptions of India were designed to preserve vested interests and structures of power. The shortcomings of Indians and those of mixed race tended to support British claims to a monopoly of responsible positions in the administration. Against the anarchy and moral and sexual degeneracy of Indian society, the British in India represented the essential virtues of Western civilization,

> peace, order, the supremacy of law, the prevention of crime, the redress of wrong, the enforcement of contracts, the development and concentration of the military force of the state, the construction of public works, the collection and expenditure of revenue required for these objects in such a way as to promote to the utmost the public interest, interfer-

ing as little as possible with the comfort, or wealth of the inhabitants . . .

Fitzjames Stephen's concept of ideal government in British India would not seem out of place in Thatcherite Britain or Ronald Reagan's America, just over a century later. Certainly, the services in India saw Stephen's formulae as ingredients of the 'rational' magic they exercised against the 'primitive' magic of those they ruled. The source of this rational magic was as supernatural as that it sought to overcome, for, as Lord Curzon proclaimed in his last speech addressed to the British before leaving India in 1905,

the Almighty has placed in your hands the greatest of His plows, in whose furrows the nations of the world are germinating and taking shape, to drive the blade a little forward in your time, and to feel that somewhere among these millions you have left a little justice or happiness or prosperity, a sense of manliness or moral dignity, a spring of patriotism, a dawn of intellectual enlightenment, or a stirring of duty, where it did not before exist—that is enough, that is the Englishman's justification in India.

But already the task had become thankless. The Indian educated-classes demonstrated their lack of gratitude in their continuing and ever shriller demands for political power. The problems of the Indian masses seemed more and more incapable of solution. The 'unchanging East' with its organic conservatism resistful of even the most worthy change became the cliché of failure.

It is symptomatic of a time of growing weariness in the rulers that the theatre of empire put on its most gaudy displays. In the 1870s, observing the peculiar attachment of the subjects of the native princes to the trappings of oriental monarchy, the British decided to adopt some of the pomp of oriental circumstance to their own use. In 1877, Queen Victoria was proclaimed Empress of India at a Durbar, a version of the traditional gathering of Indian princes, at which, in a grandiose ritual, they declared their loyalty to their sovereign. In 1903, an even more elaborate and lavish display, greeting the king-emperor Edward on his coronation, was held at Delhi, the old capital of the Mughal emperors.

It was a scene that made one catch one's breath in wonder; for those who saw it nothing will ever dim the memory of the solemn irresistible march of the elephants, the swaying howdahs of burnished gold and silver, the proud Maharajas seated on high, the clanging bells and the strains of martial music, the silent motionless enveloping troops, the uncountable crowds in radiant vestments . . .

It was only fitting 'that for sheer spectacular magnificence' no sight could be compared 'with the elephant procession of the State Entry. Pictures convey no adequate conception of the marvellous moment when the Viceroy on a gigantic elephant, with all the greatest princes of India in his train . . . entered Delhi slowly, impressively, the central figure in a vision so resplendent that at first the awestruck crowds forgot to cheer.'

From such heights there was nowhere to go but down. In the years of imperial decline, the grandiose remained, though increasingly muted. The isolation of the rulers deepened. As did the melancholy which is a side-effect of both the fear of loss and the fantasy of betrayal.

Part Three

MAKING NATIONALISTS

8

ACCEPTANCE AND COLLABORATION

'He was strangely amaz'd and surpriz'd at opening of a Bottle of Bottled Drink, when he saw it froth and fly about. The President asked him what it was struck him with such Amazement, which was not, he told him, the sight of the Drink flying out of the Bottle, but how such Liquor could ever be put in.' The Reverend Thomas Overton's anecdote (written down at the end of the seventeenth century) of an Indian merchant's experience as a guest at a European dinner, sums up the mixture of incredulity and fascination which characterizes the early effect of the West upon Indian sensibilities.

It was material things which first attracted the attention of those Indians in closest contact with the Europeans. Clocks and carriages, tables and chairs, mirrors and prints, foreign luxuries, were as easily accepted as was the collaboration necessary for the creation of mutual profit. There was no interest at that time in the deeper layers of Western culture, even if its representatives had been concerned with revealing them, which they were not. They were not secure enough in their position, and in any case it might interfere with business. The early Westerner in India was not out to peddle his own civilization and culture. On the contrary, he was usually more impressed by the civilization and culture he found there than with the one he had brought with him.

It was only much later, in the nineteenth century, when the effects of the Industrial Revolution in Britain were felt in India, that the indigenous merchant classes, now considerably more sophisticated and knowledgeable, invested in the West's technology and became industrial capitalists themselves. It was from among these Indian capitalists that the independence movement was to draw its financial backers.

The attitude of the princes and other nobles moved from condescension through apprehension to collaboration, as the British transformed themselves from traders into rulers. Their first interest, like the merchant's, was in the luxurious trivia the West had to offer. When the British began their conquest of India, the rulers, curious about how they were doing it, were more than anxious to acquire the secret. They bought European arms, and then bought Europeans to establish factories to make them. It was logical to hire European mercenaries to train and command their armies in the European manner. When finally the princes were forced to acknowledge British supremacy, they did, on the whole, accept a dependent position. Previous conquerors had been more inclined to dispose of indigenous rulers. The British were different, or so it seemed.

By the end of the nineteenth century, two-fifths of India was still divided into states ruled by native princes. The people of these territories were not British subjects and received neither the protection of British law nor that of the British parliament. The states existed because, in the early expansion of the British in India, military and political exigencies had made allies of some of the native rulers. Under various treaties, the ruling dynasties had surrendered the management of their external relations to the British Crown, but, generally speaking, they were free to rule themselves in any way they wished as long as it was neither detrimental to British interests in India nor overstepping the bounds of toleration.

At one time, before the Mutiny of 1857, it had been the policy of the Indian government to annex wherever possible the territories of native princes, and the manner in which this had been done was one of the causes of the revolt. But during the Mutiny most of the princes remained loyal, at at least neutral, and it was decided that no further annexations would take place. The princely states, some of which were only a few square miles in extent, were 562 in number and were scattered quite haphazardly all over India. The smaller states were forced to accept a large measure of British control over their administration, but the more important states were internally almost completely independent. Their relationships with the government of India operated only through the viceroy as representative of the British Crown. The states had certain obligations towards the 'Paramount Power', as the Crown was called. They were, for example, obliged to supply military forces if required for the defence of India. In the final analysis, they were not really sovereign; their internal affairs were subject to supervision and the Paramount Power could intervene even to the extent of deposing the ruler, though such intervention was very rare.

Most of the rulers of these states were Hindus, but this did not mean that their subjects were also Hindus. Kashmir, for example, had some three million Muslims and one million Hindus, but the Maharaja was a Hindu; Hyderabad, the largest of the states (slightly larger than Scotland and England put together) had a Muslim ruler, though the Muslims were outnumbered twelve to one by Hindus.

These problems were not to become matters of real consequence until the end of Empire. In the meanwhile, the rulers enjoyed their position in the hierarchy of British India. The British went to great lengths to dramatize the superficialities of power. In the theatre of the Raj, the princes were given a most colourful and exotic role. Their social precedence was carefully ordered. Salutes ranging from nine to twenty-one guns were assigned. A prince with a salute of eleven guns or more was addressed as 'His Highness'. Such honours could be used to bring pressure on individual princes. When, for example, one allowed a thief to be punished in the traditional way, by having a hand or a foot chopped off, he was deprived of his salute and fined.

Late in the nineteenth century, quite a number of princes

caused trouble. They had assimilated not only Western education, but also Western tastes. As long as the latter were
confined to the usual material trivia, no one could object. The
princes might build palaces modelled on the Petit Trianon or
on London's St Pancras station, and the viceroy would raise no
more than an eyebrow, if that. But to suggest that they might
marry a white woman was taking Westernization too far.

When the young Raja of Pudukkottai wanted to go to
England for the celebration of Queen Victoria's diamond
jubilee in 1897, the government of India would not let him go.
The reasons were many. He was extravagant. His character
was such that he would probably create a scandal. But the most
important objection was the fear that he might marry a white
woman.

The desires of the newly emerging Indian middle classes
were somewhat different to those of the princes; at least, their
priorities were. They wanted education, the key to Western
knowledge, and they wanted it in English. At first, the British
were not sure that they wanted to give it to them.

The type of education the British had found when they
arrived in India was almost entirely religious, and higher
education for Hindus and Muslims was purely literary. Hindu
higher education was almost a Brahmin monopoly. Brahmins,
the priestly caste, spent their time studying religious texts in a
dead language, Sanskrit. There were a number of schools
using living languages, but few Brahmins would send their
children to such schools, where the main subject taught was
the preparation of accounts. Muslim higher education *was*
conducted in a living language—Arabic, which was not spoken
in India. But there were also schools which taught Persian (the
official language of government in India until 1837, when it
was finally abandoned) and some secular subjects.

Hindu and Muslim systems of education had much in
common. Both used, in the main, a language unknown to
ordinary people. Both stuck firmly to traditional knowledge.

Muslim education, however, was more democratic than Hindu, for where the latter was confined almost exclusively to the Brahmin castes, the former was open to all Muslims. The State—as distinct from individual rulers—accepted no responsibility for education. Schools existed on private or community funds. As late as 1835, the ancient seat of Hindu learning at Nadia in Bengal still managed to preserve its character as a university because the local rajas endowed certain teachers with lands for the instruction and maintenance of scholars. This was not an isolated example. Muslim schools were similarly supported by Muslim rulers and communities.

By the time the British began to exercise power in Bengal, however, the general state of the country had to some extent reduced private endowments for educational institutions. The new government's first excursion into Indian education followed the traditional pattern of the country. In 1780, a Muslim teacher petitioned Warren Hastings on behalf of a number of leading Muslims and gave him the opportunity to demonstrate that the British were just as concerned with the patronage of education as their predecessors had been. In 1781, suitable quarters were found for a Muslim teacher (*maulvi*) and the Calcutta Madrasa was founded. What Hastings had done for Muslims was later to be done for Hindus. In 1792, a Sanskrit College was established at Benares, whose object was 'the preservation and cultivation of the laws, literature and religion of that nation [the Hindu] at this centre of their faith and common resort of all their tribes'. The scholars at the Sanskrit College were to be examined four times a year in the presence of the British Resident at Benares, except in such religious matters as were not supposed to be discussed in the presence of non-Brahmins. Neither the Muslim nor the Hindu institution proved successful: both were riddled with feuds, the funds were improperly used, and there were frequent reports of grave misconduct and disorder.

In 1811, as is apparent from a rather incoherent minute

(dated 6 March) of the governor-general, Lord Minto, the 'orientalist' school, made up of those who thought the Indian language should be the media of instruction, was uppermost.

It is common remark that science and literature are in a progressive state of decay amongst the natives of India . . . The number of the learned is not only diminished, but the circle of learning, even among those who still devote themselves to it, appears to be considerably contracted. The abstract sciences are abandoned, polite literature neglected, and no branch of learning cultivated but what is connected with the peculiar religious doctrines of the people. The immediate consequence of this state of things is the disuse, and even actual loss, of many valuable books; and it is to be apprehended that, unless Government interfere with a fostering hand, the revival of letters may shortly become hopeless from a want of books or of persons capable of explaining them.

Nothing was actually done until the Charter Act of 1813, when the evangelicals managed to have a clause inserted in the charter to the effect that

it shall be lawful for the governor-general-in-council to direct that . . . a sum of not less than one lakh [100,000] of rupees in each year shall be set apart and applied to the revival and improvement of literature and the encouragement of the learned natives of India, and for the introduction and promotion of a knowledge of the sciences among the inhabitants of the British territories in India.

The sum allocated was extremely small and no one seemed to have much idea about how it was to be used. The directors' instructions were, perhaps deliberately, vague and it was 1815 before Lord Moira (later Marquess of Hastings), who was governor-general from 1813 to 1824, was able to consider what action might be taken. Hastings's opinion was that there must be improvements in the education of the masses. 'The remedy', he said, 'is to furnish the village schoolmasters with little manuals of religious sentiments and ethic maxims conveyed in such a shape as may be attractive to the scholars, taking care that while awe and adoration of the Supreme Being are earnestly instilled, no jealousy be excited by pointing out any particular creed.' There were other equally woolly suggestions for helping institutions of higher learning. The directors ignored them all, and for some years the education allocation was not disbursed.

Though the government appeared incapable of formulating any educational policy, private individuals and organizations were anxious to establish schools. They, unlike the government, wanted to provide Western education in the English language—which, though not explicitly stated, had been the intention behind the clause in the Charter Act of 1813. In 1817, a number of Indians and British established the Calcutta School Book Society and the Hindu College. Their example was followed by others, and more schools teaching English were established, some sponsored by missionaries, others by Indians. Their motives differed. Most Indians saw English education as a passport to official appointments and as a tool of commerce. The missionaries, on the other hand, saw it as a means of conversion through which the Indians 'now engaged in the degrading and polluting worship of idols shall be brought to the knowledge of the true God and Jesus Christ whom He has sent'.

The government's slowness in implementing the educational clause of the 1813 Charter Act was due partly to security considerations—for it believed that it was a dangerous policy to interfere in any way with traditional patterns of Indian society—and partly to the pressures of 'orientalist' opinion. It still did not consider it to be the government's duty to sponsor

English education. In 1823 it established a General Committee of Public Instruction, whose function was to take charge of existing government educational institutions and to administer the educational grant. The committee was further to enquire into the educational situation and to advise on measures for the better instruction of the people and the 'improvement of their moral character'. But the committee soon found itself overwhelmed by its task. Taking the easy way out, it decided to spend the allocation on supporting Sanskrit and Arabic learning. There was considerable opposition to the government's decision in 1823 to found and support a new college for Sanskrit studies. Ram Mohun Roy, the Bengali reformer, in a letter to the governor-general, expressed the sentiments of those who wanted the intellectual and material advantages which would result from their being given access to 'mathematics, natural philosophy, chemistry, anatomy, and other useful sciences, which the natives of Europe have carried to a degree of perfection that has raised them above the inhabitants of other parts of the world'. They were, Ram Mohun continued, horrified at the idea that they were to receive instead a school which could 'only be expected to load the minds of youth with grammatical niceties and metaphysical distinctions of little or no practical use to the possessors or to society'. If it was the government's policy to 'keep this country in darkness', establishing a Sanskrit college was the best way of going about it. But this and other protests had no effect. It was the committee's opinion that 'tuition in European sciences [is] neither among the sensible wants of the people nor in the power of the government to bestow.'

The committee were fighting a losing battle. Not only was there a general desire among Indians—particularly in Bengal—for English education, but the influence of reformers and political thinkers in Britain was behind it too. The famous missionary, Dr Duff, recalled that in Calcutta 'the excitement for Western education continued unabated. They pursued us along the streets; they threw open the doors of our palankeens; they poured in their supplications with a pitiful earnestness of countenance which might have softened a heart of stone.'

The stone was already softening, and for sound ideological reasons. Lord William Bentinck, already engaged in a number of reforms, wrote to the Committee of Public Instruction on 26 June 1829.

Impressed with a deep conviction of the importance of the subject, and cordially disposed to promote the great object of improving India by spreading abroad the lights of European knowledge, morals, and civilisation, his Lordship in Council has no hesitation in stating to your Committee and in authorising you to announce to all concerned in the superintendence of your native seminaries that it is the wish and admitted policy of the British Government to render its own language gradually and eventually the language of public business throughout the country, and that it will omit no opportunity of giving every reasonable and practical degree of encouragement to the execution of this project.

The committee at this time was evenly divided between 'orientalists' and anglicizers. While they debated, private initiative continued to expand the number of schools teaching the English language and Western subjects. The 'orientalists' were, in fact, losing ground. Their essentially conservative attitude was quite alien to the new spirit which permeated Britain's view of her responsibilities in India. When T. B. Macaulay arrived in India, this spirit—already expressed by Bentinck—received powerful reinforcement. Macaulay's Education Minute of 1835 summed up the reformist attitude. The decision to make English the medium of higher education was announced in a brief resolution on 7 March 1835. 'His Lordship is of the opinion', said the first paragraph of the resolution, 'that the great object of the British Government ought to be the promotion of European literature and science among the natives of India, and that all the funds appropriated for the purpose of education would be best employed on English education alone.'

The decision to divert government funds to the provision of English education alone not only satisfied the demands of the growing Hindu middle classes but also met the fundamental problems of the economy. The government's resources were strictly limited. The cost of any project to translate textbooks into Indian languages, for example, would have been ruinously expensive. All practical considerations were in favour of using English textbooks. The same considerations demanded that the scope of education should be limited, though it was hoped that knowledge could be diffused. Once certain sections of the population had been given an English education, the government thought, they would be able to pass on the knowledge they had acquired to their countrymen—in their own languages. Macaulay's brother-in-law, Charles Trevelyan, wrote:

The rich, the learned, the men of business, will first be gained. A new class of teachers will be trained; books in the vernacular language will be multiplied; and with these accumulated means we shall in due time proceed to extend our operations from town to country, from the few to the many, until every hamlet shall be provided with its elementary school. The poor man is not less the object of the committee's solicitude than the rich; but, while the means at their disposal were extremely limited, there were millions of all classes to be educated. It was absolutely necessary to make a selection, and they therefore selected the upper and middle classes as the first object of their attention, because, by educating them first, they would soonest be able to extend the same advantages to the rest of the people.

The decision to concentrate on providing Western education in the English language was made from motives other than economy, though that was undoubtedly of first importance. But education had moral, political and commercial overtones in the eyes of such men as Macaulay. He, and those who thought like him, were following evangelical rather than utilitarian principles. It was Charles Grant who was the prophet of English education in India, not James Mill. Indeed, Mill was highly sceptical about the effectiveness of *any* form of education in India. The moral overtones were, of course, Christian in character. They were reflected by Macaulay in a letter to his father in 1836, in which he forecast that in thirty years' time there would be not a single idolater among the respectable classes in Bengal, a situation which would be brought about merely by the diffusion of knowledge.

That many Indians were aware that there was a proselytizing purpose behind English education had been shown in their suspicion when such education was offered by missionaries. Bishop's College, for example, which had been established in Calcutta in 1820, would not admit non-Christians; its real function was to create missionaries who would go out and evangelize the heathen. It never attracted more than eleven scholars at any one time during the twenty-five years following its establishment. Though great pressure was brought to bear on the government, from both Britain and India, to introduce religious instruction into government schools, it refused to depart from its traditional neutrality in matters of religion until 1854, by which time it had become clear that Macaulay's hopes for conversion-by-example had not been realized. The moral motive also had a more immediate and practical application. Following the administrative reforms, a growing number of Indians were joining government service, with increasing responsibility and powers, particularly in the judicial and revenue branches. English education was intended to make them morally and intellectually 'fit' to perform their duties with efficiency and probity.

The commercial motive was also extremely powerful, and it gained for the cause of English education the full support of the mercantile community in Calcutta as well as in Britain. The economic activities of the British had already produced a commercial middle class in India, on whose collaboration the expansion of the economy depended. Collaboration was needed not only for exploiting India's natural resources; it was essential to the creation of that prosperity which would lead to the purchase and consumption of British goods. To people who thought in these terms, commerce was more important than conquest. Macaulay, who is so frequently the mouthpiece of his times, put the case in his great speech in the House of Commons on the Charter Act of 1833.

The mere extent of empire is not necessarily an advantage. To many governments it has been cumbersome; to some it has been fatal. It will be allowed by every statesman of our time that the prosperity of a country is made up of the prosperity of those who compose the community, and that it is the most childish ambition to covet dominion which adds to no man's comfort or security . . . It would be, on the most selfish view of the case, far better for us that the people of India were well-governed and independent of us, than ill-governed and subject to us; that they were ruled by their own kings, but wearing our broadcloth, and working with our cutlery, than that they were performing their salaams to English collectors and English magistrates *but were too ignorant to value*, or too poor to buy English manufactures.

Of course, Macaulay, and others who thought like him, did not anticipate that Indians would be demanding their inde-

Lord Macaulay, historian, poet and statesman (1800–1859)

Sir John Lawrence in conference in India, 1863. Lawrence is seated, centre, Lord Napier is seated on his left.

Proclamation of Queen Victoria as Empress of India at Delhi, 1877

The Viceroy, Lord Curzon, and Lady Curzon, right, and the Duke and
Duchess of Connaught, left, mounting their elephants, December 29th,
1902

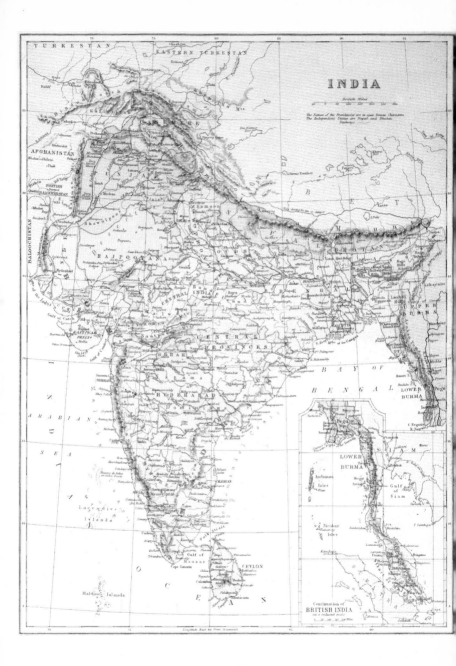

Map of India

Lord Dufferin and Ava, painted by G. F. Watts

M. K. Gandhi, the lawyer, sits outside his office in South Africa.

Gandhi with his wife, Kasturba, after his return from South Africa

pendence in the foreseeable future. Neither did Indians, certainly those who wished to acquire the apparent boons of Western civilization. On the contrary, they began to see themselves in the position that at first appeared to be allotted to them by the British rulers: partners, with a reversion upon the whole.

In some areas of the administration, the Western-educated classes became partners, though very junior ones, with a part to play in the decision-making process. This was in the lower levels of the Civil Service. There was, however, one area in which they could play an essential role: the administration of justice.

Though pre-British India had its systems of law and legal institutions, both Hindu and Muslim, they had, generally speaking, ceased to function or had been distorted by the operation of irresponsible force during the collapse of the Mughal Empire. The village *panchayat*, the most widely surviving judicial institution, had no precise code of law, and its actions were governed by customs and precedents which were often purely local in character and acceptance. In the strict sense, the *panchayat* was a court not of law but of arbitration. It functioned only with the consent of those involved in a dispute, and had no powers of enforcement. Nevertheless, it did have certain techniques of coercion. One of these was known as *dharna*. The injured party would fast on the other party's doorstep, on the principle that if the man fasting died, his death was the responsibility of the other and would bring the wrath of the gods down upon him. It was a technique adapted by Gandhi for his own purposes.

Coexisting with Hindu law was the Islamic system which had been introduced into India by the Mughal conquerors. The civil system applied only to Muslims and was never at any time imposed on Hindus. Like Hindu law, it was mainly concerned with personal relations—marriage, property and so on. But, under the Mughals, Muslim *criminal* law applied to both Muslims and Hindus. By and large, in the eighteenth century, the Muslim penal code was far more enlightened than English law. The death penalty was rarely imposed, at a time when in England it was the punishment for over 150 offences. The Mughals, however, made no attempt to develop an organized system of law designed to regulate disputes between members of the two principal religious communities in India, nor did there exist any machinery of justice—for there was no law of evidence, or of procedure.

The first concern of the British when they came to establish their rule was to organize the administration of justice. The foundations were laid during the government of Warren Hastings in Bengal and, with modifications, the system then established survived until the end of British rule. Hastings's first principle was that courts should be open to all, whatever their religion. Such courts were set up in the administrative areas known as 'districts', and two other courts, civil and criminal, were created to act as courts of appeal. They administered English law, but their jurisdiction was limited at first to Calcutta, Bombay and Madras. Furthermore, to Indians they were required to apply customary law, either Hindu or Muslim. This dual system of law, English and customary, was maintained until 1861.

After 1861, there was a considerable expansion of the areas covered by Western-style civil and criminal law. This was welcomed by the majority of middle-class Indians because it gave them firstly the protection of written law, and secondly, a dominant role in interpreting it to a largely illiterate population. The practice of the law offered both an opportunity for employment and at least a measure of participation in the structure of power. In fact, the British could not do without them.

It was not only within those parts of India directly ruled by the British that the study of Western law offered an avenue to success. On the death of the then prime minister of the little princely state of Rajkot, his family decided that with English legal qualifications his son would have a better chance to follow in his footsteps. Failing that, he could set himself up in lucrative practice. In 1888, Mohandas Karamchand Gandhi, not quite nineteen years old, boarded a ship at Bombay for London. In doing so, he flouted the wishes of his caste community, who promptly excommunicated him.

9

ENVY AND REJECTION

Envy, frustration and rejection are stages in the growth of colonial nationalism, but the foundation is self-interest.

The first political organization in British India was formed in 1837 and took the name of the Landowners' Association in the following year. Though the organizers claimed that the association was intended to 'embrace people of all descriptions, without reference to caste, country or complexion', it was a special-interest group designed to defend landlords against what was believed to be the pro-peasant bias of the British government.

The association received support from a number of Englishmen and from the British India Society which was founded in London in 1839. They suggested that the name gave the impression of much too sectional an interest. In 1843, an entirely new organization, the Bengal British India Society, was founded. Its objects were to be

the collection and dissemination of information relating to the actual condition of the people of British India, and the laws and institutions, and resources of the country, and to employ such other means of peaceable and lawful character as may appear calculated to secure the welfare, extend the just rights, and advance the interests of all classes of our fellow subjects.

The meeting at which the society was constituted pledged its loyalty to Britain and disclaimed any desire to 'subvert legal authority or disturb the peace and well-being of society'. The

Landholders' Association maintained its separate existence, but by 1851 both organizations were moribund.

In that year, a new body, the British Indian Association, was formed, partly to channel protest against legal discriminations and partly to make representations to the British government when the Company's charter came up for renewal in 1853. The association professed to welcome all classes, but the subscription was so high that only the wealthier could afford it. The association was—and remained—an upper-class body representing powerful landholding and merchant interests. Branches were soon established in Madras, Poona and Bombay. The association memorialized the government on almost every conceivable subject, though it was fundamentally concerned with the removal of discriminatory tariffs and the admittance of Indians to the legislatures and the civil administration.

At the first annual general meeting of the Bombay branch, one speaker made a prophetic speech:

> The British government professes to educate the Natives to an equality with Europeans, an object worthy of the age and of Britain. But if Englishmen after educating the Natives to be their equals continue to treat them as their inferiors—if they deny the stimulus to honourable ambition, and show the Natives that there is a barrier over which superior Native merit and ambition can never hope to pass, and that these are considered traits which a Native cannot hope to exhibit —are they not in effect undoing all that they have done, unteaching the Native all that he has been taught, and pursuing a suicidal policy, which will inevitably array all the talent, honour, and intelligence of the country ultimately in irreconcilable hostility to the ruling power?

These first political associations represented moderate and gradualist views, but by the end of Company rule there was a growing sense of frustration among the educated middle classes. The younger elements among the Western-educated were beginning to turn away from wholehearted identification with Western ideas and ambitions, and the alienation from traditional society to which such identification inevitably led. They were moving towards a new sense of being Indian—or, more precisely, of being Hindu.

At this time there was no real concept of an *Indian* nationalism in the geographic or ethnic sense. This was mainly because British dominion did not spread throughout India until just before the Mutiny. Linguistic and cultural differences, too, separated the various parts of the country from each other. Modern communications did not exist, and there was little exchange of ideas between the intelligentsia of the provinces of British India. When there was, its effect was confined to a minority of the urban middle classes in the provincial capitals. Bengali nationalism, however, *was* taking root, and so was a particularly Hindu nationalism. This was not unnatural; the majority of the Western-educated were in fact Hindus. The Muslims were basically indifferent to the West, and their indifference was reinforced not only by their religion but by the fact that they had been dispossessed from their rule by the British. Generally speaking, they lived withdrawn from the effects of Westernization, though this was to change after 1858.

By the end of Company rule, the main attitudes which nationalism was to take in India already existed. All were responses to Western influences, and even those which appeared totally to reject Western ideas and values were motivated by them. All were attempts to declare some sort of identity, either in the conqueror's terms or in those of indigenous religions and cultures. In a very real sense, the Mutiny cleared the decks, crystallized emotions, and laid down the order of battle.

The promise in Queen Victoria's proclamation of November 1858 'so far as may be, our subjects, of whatever race or creed, be freely and impartially admitted to office in our service, the duties of which they may be qualified by their education, ability, and integrity duly to discharge', was designed primarily to heal the wounds of the Mutiny, and it had naturally raised expectations among the Indian middle classes; in practice it was denied, and on purely racial grounds. Most educated Indians had looked to government employment as a reward for their anglicization. Their purely literary education, in fact, fitted them for no other. The discrimination against them was therefore an economic one as well.

Racial—and therefore cultural—discrimination inevitably led to religious revivalism. Economic and political discrimination led both to moderation and extremism, to imitative ideologies and to Hindu nationalism. During most of the latter part of the nineteenth century, these two aspects of Indian reaction remained separate, but by the beginning of the twentieth century, they had come together.

A third attitude—the desire to create some form of synthesis between Eastern and Western ethical values, first propounded by Ram Mohun Roy in the early part of the nineteenth century—influenced both sides. Ram Mohun founded the Brahmo Samaj ('Society of the Worshippers of God') and its work was continued after his death, first by Debendranath Tagore (1817–1905), father of the poet and Nobel laureate Rabindranath Tagore, and then by Keshab Chandra Sen (1839–84). Debendranath sought to continue the purification of Hinduism which had been begun by Ram Mohun, while Keshab tried to create a genuine synthesis between Hinduism and Christianity. The Brahmo Samaj influenced only a very small minority of Indians, but its role under both Debendranath and Keshab was seminal, for it helped to fashion the religious understanding of such men as Rabindranath Tagore and Mahatma Gandhi.

The activities of Debendranath and Keshab were primarily

[135]

defensive. Those of Dayananda Saraswati (1824–83), however, were aggressive and full of Hindu self-confidence. Dayananda rejected Western ideas and proposed, instead of a synthesis, the revival of the old religion of the Aryans who had invaded India around 1500 BC and whose sacred books, the *Vedas*, were the foundation of Hinduism. Dayananda's teaching was revolutionary, for it claimed that there was no Vedic authority for most of the customs of Hindu society —rigidity of caste, untouchability, or child marriage. In 1875, he founded in Bombay the Arya Samaj ('Society of Noble Men').

To many orthodox Hindus, the members of the Brahmo Samaj—the 'Brahmos', as they were called—seemed distinctly irreligious. Their attacks on Hinduism as a religion in need of reform seemed to be a capitulation to Western critics. Many Brahmos did, indeed, express contempt for several aspects of Indian life. They were themselves fully Westernized in their general behaviour. If they had chosen to become Christians (although very few educated Indians were, in fact, converted), orthodox Hindus could have ignored them. But they did not, and their desire to reform Hinduism by assimilating Western ideas appeared to be designed to subvert the very foundations of Hindu society.

In the eyes of most Hindus, the government of India *could not be* a secular government. In Hinduism, there is no divorce between religion and society. According to this reasoning, the British government of India was a Christian government. Whatever its disclaimers, its aim was assumed to be total conversion of Indians to Western ideas, both social and religious. Orthodox Hindus saw the Brahmos as secret agents, preparing the ground by undermining Hinduism in order to make way for Christian missionaries. So, too, the moderates' demand for political reform was viewed as an attempt to entrench in the system those who most approved of that system. If Westernized Indians became involved in the process of government, they would have a hand in further reforming legislation. There seemed, in this, to be an overt threat to orthodox Hinduism.

It was implicit in Dayananda's desire to cleanse Hinduism that it should be revitalized and so become a force which might resist Westernizing tendencies. But there was more to the aims of the Arya Samaj than that. The British had imposed on traditional Indian society a vast superstructure of Western law, economic organization and administration. Whatever ortho-dox religious leaders believed, the government after the Mutiny had no intention of taking aggressive action, overt or clandestine, against the traditional social order. But Western systems, in themselves, were continuously assaulting long-held customs and attitudes to life. For orthodox Hindus, there was no possibility of reconciliation. Cultural and religious freedom, they believed, could be achieved only through poli-tical freedom. As a contemporary Englishman put it, the logic of Dayananda's view was that 'the religion of India as well as the sovereignty of India ought to belong to the Indian people; in other words, Indian religion for the Indians, Indian sovereignty for the Indians.'

Another stage in what might be called the rehabilitation of Hinduism was represented by Ramakrishna Paramahamsa (1836–86) and by his disciple and propagandist, Vivekananda (1862–1902). To traditional Hinduism they added the ideas of social service and of self-reliance. Vivekananda's appeals on behalf of the downtrodden masses gave nationalist leaders an opportunity to express, in political terms, the demands not just of a minority but of the majority of India's people. In his response to these appeals, Gandhi, in the twentieth century, helped to give the nationalist movement an apparently broad base of resistance to British rule. Vivekananda's rousing speeches to the young men of India, urging them to dedicate themselves to changing the lives of millions of their poor and starving fellow-countrymen, were to give nationalist sentiment a sense not only of reality but of purpose—and of a purpose entirely Indian in character.

Hindu self-confidence was further bolstered by the work of the Theosophical Society founded in New York in 1875 by the Russian spiritualist, Madame Blavatsky. The society's wholehearted acceptance of Hinduism was expressed in a pseudo-intellectual manner which had considerable appeal for Indians repelled by the emotionalism of Ramakrishna and Vivekananda. One such was the thirteen-year-old, Jawaharlal Nehru, who, in 1902, became so interested in the teachings of the Theosophists that to the amusement of his highly Wester-nized father, he was initiated into the Theosophical Society by no less a person than Madame Blavatsky's successor, Mrs Annie Besant, who later chose to be active in Indian politics.

In the nineteenth century, however, none of these move-ments specified, or even advocated, political action. What they did was supply a series of ideas and emotions which had to wait for a political vocabulary in which they might be expressed, as well as for leaders capable of using that vocabulary. Mean-while, the moderate elements—the liberals, the gradualists, the hopeful co-operators with the British—continued to found quasi-political movements designed to persuade the British to grant liberal institutions to India, institutions through which these moderates could play a part in the government of their country. Whatever their political platforms, such movements still tended to represent the limited interests of the educated classes. The moderate leaders were, generally speaking, men with a secular outlook who believed that religion could be separated from politics. And, despite everything, they con-tinued to believe in the fundamental good faith of British intentions. Every time the British denied them the right to appointments at the higher levels of the Civil Service, they hid their embarrassment and, in their weakness, removed them-selves even further from contact with the Indian masses.

Nevertheless, the moderates played an extremely important

role in developing the Westernizing strand in the complex pattern of Indian nationalism. In their attempt to find in Western society a spur for Indian action, they looked to a wider field than English liberalism. They saw, in mid-nineteenth-century Europe, examples of men who challenged the old order of things. Garibaldi, Mazzini and the others who formed the Young Italy movement inspired some of them with great hopes. They pointed to patriotism and to nationalism, in its European sense, as great and vital forces.

Again, the initiative came from Bengal. The British Indian Association was so obviously a class-oriented association that the middle classes felt it unsuitable for the expression of their interests. A number of Bengalis suggested that a strictly Bengali organization should be formed, but this was thought to be too parochial. An attempt was made to force the British Indian Association to open itself to a wider membership by reducing its subscription, but this was not successful. In 1875, a new organization, the India League, was formed in Calcutta to co-ordinate the activities of a number of district associations. Its aims were

> to ascertain and propagate the views of the people as to how Indians could progress in the political and other fields; to discuss and adopt the means which we should consider proper for the good of our countrymen and for the diffusion of political education amongst them; to devise and adopt legitimate means for safeguarding the interests of different classes; to stimulate the spirit of nationalism among the people; to adopt means for the development of economic resources of the country.

The subscription (five rupees) was a tenth of what the British Indian Association asked, and artisans, cultivators and village headmen could join for a special subscription of one rupee—which was still, however, quite a large sum.

A year after the India League was formed, another organization, the Indian Association, was also founded in Calcutta.
Among those present was Surendranath Banerjea (1848–
1926), who had been one of the first Indians admitted to the
Indian Civil Service but who had been dismissed in 1874 for
what the secretary of state for India described as 'a palpable
misuse of his judicial powers' and for being 'guilty of false-
hood'. In fact, he had failed to correct a false report by a
subordinate—a crime for which his English colleagues would
have received no more than a departmental reprimand. Surendranath's appeal, when he presented himself in London, was
dismissed, and he returned to India convinced that 'the personal wrong to me was an illustration of the impotency of our
people.' He determined to dedicate the rest of his life to
'redressing our wrongs and protecting our rights, personal and
collective'.

The idea of a truly all-India organization was very much in
the minds of the men present at the founding of the Indian
Association in 1876, 'for even then,' wrote Banerjea, 'the
conception of a united India, derived from the inspiration of
Mazzini, or, at any rate, of bringing all India upon the same
common political platform, had taken firm possession of the
minds of the Indian leaders in Bengal.' An immediate attempt
was made to identify the Indian Association with popular
causes. The first crusade took up the complaint of third-class
railway passengers at not having lavatories in the coaches. The
association's agitation was successful.

The association held its first public meeting in March 1877
to protest at discrimination against Indian candidates for the
Indian Civil Service. The age limit had been lowered from
twenty-one to nineteen, and it was suggested at the meeting
that examinations for the service should be held simultaneously in Britain and India, and not—as was the practice—in
Britain alone. At the same meeting, Surendranath Banerjea
was appointed as a special delegate whose duty was to visit

other parts of India. He left Calcutta in May 1877 for an extended tour, during which he spoke at many public meetings. Surendranath made considerable impact on his audiences. It was necessary, he said at a meeting in 1878, to preach

the great doctrine of peace and good will between Hindus and Musulmans, Christians and Parsees, aye between all sections of the great Indian community. Let us raise aloft the banner of our country's progress. Let the word 'Unity' be inscribed there in characters of glittering gold . . . There may be religious differences between us. There may be social differences between us. But there is a common platform where we may all meet, the platform of our country's welfare.

Under Surendranath's influence, a number of organizations were established in different parts of India, designed to act in concert with the Indian Association.

The association continued to agitate against discriminatory actions by the government. In 1880, it even sent a representative to Britain to help appeal to the electorate on behalf of the Libral Party, in which many Indians had placed their hopes of a new deal.

In 1883, the Indian Association took advantage of an industrial exhibition in Calcutta to arrange a national conference, hoping to attract some of the many leading Indians who were expected in the city for the occasion. Early in the same year, Surendranath Banerjea had been imprisoned for two months on a charge of contempt of court, and this had brought his name to the attention of a wider public. But when the 'national' conference took place, it was still very much a local affair, three-quarters of the delegates coming from Bengal. Much emphasis was placed on the desirability of parliamentary government for India, and one speaker—the English writer, Wilfred Scawen Blunt—noted at the end of the conference:

'So ended the first session of the Indian Parliament. May it be memorable in history.'

The Indian Association held its second meeting in Calcutta in 1885. At the same time, another body was holding its first meeting in Bombay. This was the Indian National Congress, which was to lead the country to independence.

Congress had its origin not so much in the spontaneous desires of Indians as in the considered policy of the government. After the disturbing events of Lord Ripon's administration—particularly the British community's success in resisting legislation to permit Europeans to be tried by Indian judges —there were signs of considerable unease amongst educated Indians. The Indian Association had protested vigorously against the government's capitulation in face of Civil Service and British community disapproval. To educated Indians, it seemed as if even a Liberal viceroy was helpless against the conservatism of the British in India. The proposed bill, known as the Ilbert Bill (after the law member, Sir Courtenay Ilbert), aroused both sides to such an extent that the British-owned Calcutta newspaper, *The Englishman*, declared: 'We are on the eve of a crisis which will try the power of the British government in a way in which it has not been tried since the Mutiny of 1857.'

When Lord Dufferin arrived as viceroy in 1884, his first task was to try to quieten the unrest caused by Ripon's well-intentioned but basically weak administration. Dufferin soon developed a dislike for educated Indians. 'I have already discovered', he wrote to the secretary of state for India in February 1885, 'that the Bengalee Baboo is a most irritating and troublesome gentleman, and I entirely agree with you in thinking that we must not show ourselves at all afraid of him. He has a great deal of Celtic perverseness, vivacity and cunning, and seems to be now employed in setting up the machinery for a repeal agitation, something on the lines of O'Connell's [Irish] Patriotic Associations.' Dufferin preferred

to try to win the co-operation of the landed and other conservative elements.

Something, however, had to be done in another direction.
The tendency towards political association among the predominantly Hindu middle classes demanded some form of
neutralizing encouragement. The actual degree of government
involvement in the birth of the Indian National Congress is,
however, the subject of considerable controversy. The moving
spirit was a former civil servant, Allan Octavian Hume, and it
has been suggested that he and Lord Dufferin were entirely
responsible. But there is no satisfactory evidence for this.
There seems little doubt, however, that Dufferin welcomed
Hume's idea of 'a safety valve for the escape of great and
growing forces, generated by our own actions', and gave the
proposal his support.

Hume himself, it is claimed, was motivated by having seen in
the government's intelligence archives seven large volumes
containing reports from all over India relating to the state of
unrest. According to a memorandum allegedly preserved in
Hume's papers:

Innumerable entries referred to the secretion of old swords,
spears and matchlocks, which would be ready when required. It was not supposed that the immediate result in its
initial stages would be a revolt against our Government, or a
revolt at all in the proper sense of the word. What was
predicted was a sudden, violent outbreak of sporadic crimes,
murders of obnoxious persons, robbery of bankers, looting
of bazaars. In the existing state of the lowest half-starving
classes, it was considered that the first few crimes would be
the signal for hundreds of similar ones, and for a general
development of lawlessness, paralysing the authorities and
the respectable classes. It was considered certain also, that
everywhere the small bands would begin to coalesce into
large ones, like drops of water on a leaf; that all the bad

characters in the country would join, and that very soon after the bands obtained formidable proportions, a certain small number of the educated classes, at the time desperately, perhaps unreasonably, bitter against the Government, would join the movement, assume here and there the lead, give the outbreak cohesion and direct it as a national revolt.

If such evidence actually did exist—and no one else ever admitted to having seen it—Hume's desire to divert the educated classes towards a gradualist attitude could have been motivated by purely liberal and humanitarian feelings. The memory of the Mutiny was still strong in India, and no right-thinking person wanted a repetition of it. But, as such a view coincided with British self-interest, a machiavellian interpretation has been put upon it.

Any organization which polarized moderate and basically 'loyal' opinion was desirable from the government's point of view. Dufferin and many others were fully aware that, in a fundamentally divided society, there was really no need for the British to initiate division. All classes of Indians—and the middle classes were no exception—would do it for them. Intercommunal and interclass antagonisms were self-perpetuating. The government's real concern was to minimize violence and it seems very unlikely that, in 1885, it really considered it possible for the educated classes (already thoroughly alienated from the masses) actually to take control of a basically agrarian rebellion, as Hume suggested. However, in the face of growing revivalist tendencies amongst Hindus, it was obviously sensible to encourage organizations of moderates. The government's policy was to maintain, and if possible extend, the division between moderates and extremists.

The first meeting of the Indian National Congress took place in Bombay in December 1885. The names of seventy-two delegates were recorded, though more were probably present, including some Muslims. When the session of 1886 came, however, the secretaries of two Muslim bodies—the Mohammedan Association, founded in Calcutta in 1856, and the Central Mohammedan Association, founded in 1877— refused to attend. Basically, the Muslims were not antagonistic to Congress, merely indifferent to it. This attitude, however, did not last for long.

Syed Ahmed Khan, leader of the educated Muslims, founded in 1888 the United Indian Patriotic Association, whose primary aim was to combat the influence of Congress. One of its objects was 'to strengthen the British Rule, and to remove those bad feelings from the hearts of the Indian people which the supporters of Congress are stirring up throughout the country, and by which great dissatisfaction is being raised among the people against the British Government'. The majority of its members were Muslims and it expressed its anti-Congress feelings with a distinctly anti-Hindu bias, though this was justified by members on the grounds that Congress was directed by Bengalis, who were antagonistic to Muslims. Syed Ahmed's principal fear was that the pressure for democratic institutions would lead to the Muslim minority being dominated by the Hindu majority.

The attempts made to persuade Muslims not to support Congress were, however, none too successful. At the Congress session of 1888, there were 222 Muslims out of a total of 1,248 delegates. Congress Muslims, too, were strongly antagonistic to Syed Ahmed, whose main purpose was to keep Muslims *out* of politics and to withhold their support from the democratic, liberal and fundamentally secular aims voiced by Congress. Syed Ahmed did not really fear the organized middle classes —only that they might be successful in persuading the government to grant democratic institutions, which would then, he thought, be used by extremist Hindus to discriminate against Muslims.

Unfortunately, there was enough evidence of Hindu revivalism to confirm his worst fears. The activities of Swami Dayananda and others had distinctly anti-Muslim overtones, especially after the Cow Protection Society was established in 1882. This was directed against Muslims, who ate beef, as well as against Christians and the government which permitted the slaughter of cows. But Dayananda did not openly take religion into politics. That was left to others.

As in the case of most aspects of political action in India, the seeds of Hindu nationalism were first sown in Bengal. The novels of Bankim Chandra Chatterjee, who had been one of the two students to graduate from the new Calcutta University in 1858, supplied some of the inspiration. Bankim Chandra was a member of the Civil Service until 1891. It is a comment on the limitation placed on Indians in government service that he was appointed only as deputy magistrate and that he never advanced in rank.

Bankim Chandra wrote in Bengali, using English literary forms. In his work, he praised Hindu religious sentiments and glorified the Hindu past. His poem, 'Bande Materam' ('Hail to the Mother'), became the anthem—the 'Marseillaise', even —of Hindu nationalism, identifying love of the mother country with love of God. Though for Bankim Chandra the motherland was Bengal, it soon came to mean India and, specifically, Hindu India. In his novel, *Anandamath* (*Abbey of Bliss*), he claimed that British rule was the essential prelude to a revival of Hinduism. Bankim Chandra Chatterjee was the prophet —and, in a sense, the ideologue—of cultural and religious nationalism, and his work profoundly influenced the young Bengalis who were to turn to terrorism as their form of nationalist expression.

This looking backwards to see a reflection of the future was at the base of the ideas of the man who was to unite religious sentiment with positive political action. He was not a Bengali, but a Maratha, a member of the race which had resisted British expansion at the beginning of the nineteenth century as it had resisted the Mughals in the seventeenth. Bal Gangadhar Tilak

(1856–1920) had received a Western-style education at the Deccan College in Poona. His reading was wide, taking in most of the Hindu classics as well as the works of Hegel, Kant, Mill, Bentham, Voltaire and Rousseau. He was early determined to take up a political career and believed that the way to acquire most influence was to establish schools where patriotism and sacrifice could be taught. He had no objection to Western science, but believed that it should be absorbed and restated in Hindu terms.

For a time, Tilak co-operated with moderate elements in Bombay but, realizing that they had no mass support, he soon turned his attention to creating it for himself. He acquired a newspaper, the *Kesari* (*Lion*), and through it began to promote two new annual festivals, one dedicated to the Hindu god Ganesha—known in western India, where he was held in particular esteem, as Ganapati—and the other honouring the Maratha hero, Sivaji, who had been the most consistent opponent of the Mughal Empire. Both festivals were obviously anti-Muslim. The Sivaji festival was given even more point by the fact that it was held at the same time as the Muslim religious festival of Muhurram.

Tilak's propaganda activities and the spread of cow protection societies helped to cause considerable unease. In the North-West Provinces in 1893, there was Hindu rioting in certain districts and British troops had to be called out to restore order. Soon, there were similar riots in Bombay. There was a great deal of violent writing in vernacular newspapers. In 1897, Tilak used the intensive actions of plague officers to arouse Hindu feelings.

Bubonic plague had swept Bombay, killing some 20,000 people, and in the spring of 1897 the scourge spread through the countryside until it reached Poona. There the plague commissioners adopted determined and brutal measures—exactly what the situation required. Unfortunately, they carried them out without giving any explanation or attempting to involve the people themselves in implementing them. The chief plague officer—one Mr Rand, who was the assistant collector of Poona—used British troops to destroy property which was believed to be contaminated. It was arranged that men, women and children from infected areas should be segregated into special camps. While searching houses for people infected with the disease, the soldiers damaged shrines, sometimes looted property and frequently sent off to camps people who were in fact free from the plague. To the people of Poona, already unnerved by the hideous epidemic, Rand and his men seemed to be engaged on a senseless reign of terror. Plague commissioners came to be dreaded more than the plague itself. The rich fled the city, and panic and alarm roamed the streets.

Tilak protested against what Rand and his men—this 'vast engine of oppression', as he called them—were doing. He warned the authorities that popular resentment was running high. 'What people on earth, however docile,' he thundered in the *Kesari*, 'will continue to submit to this sort of mad terror?' In June 1897, Rand and his assistant were shot dead. A few weeks later, Tilak was arrested on a charge of sedition and, after a travesty of a trial, sentenced to eighteen months' imprisonment.

The news of Tilak's 'martyrdom' spread throughout India, and his ideas became known to a large number of that new class of young, partly Western-educated Indians who were suffering acutely from economic and social frustration. Religious nationalism had a very wide appeal. It gave to the Brahmins —the highest caste and, consequently, the natural leaders of the Hindu community—a vocabulary with which to resist the challenge to their traditional social and political influence, which was implicit in British rule. It offered the unemployed middle classes an outlet for their economic despair as well as a firm anchor within the traditional order from which their education had seemed to cut them loose. In the case of the peasants, the new nationalism mobilized the very gods of the

Hindu pantheon in their defence and encouraged them to participate in a kind of religious crusade. And to young hot-heads it offered the excitement of violence, of action rather than words.

Nevertheless, religious nationalism had little appeal for those members of the middle classes—the doctors, the lawyers, the schoolmasters and businessmen—who were members of Congress and, after the Councils Act of 1892, of the legislative councils. Generally speaking, these men had little sympathy for the peasant and his troubles. It is an interesting fact that, throughout the whole period of the struggle for freedom, a large proportion of moderate nationalists came from the legal profession; their respect for the law reinforced other pressures in favour of legitimate means of agitation. By 1899, according to a confidential government report, almost 40 per cent (5,442) of the 13,839 delegates to the Indian National Congress were from the legal profession. The other large groups consisted of 2,629 representing landed interests, and 2,091 from the commercial classes. The remainder was made up almost entirely of journalists, doctors and teachers.

Congress, like the British Indian Association, was opposed to any reform of tenants' rights, for although the legal profession might be indifferent to landlord and peasant alike, much of the financial support for Congress came from large landed proprietors. The commercial classes formed another interested party. They felt themselves oppressed, and believed that British rule did not favour indigenous capitalists. They were only partly right because, though British rule undoubtedly favoured British business undertakings, and did not actively encourage the growth of indigenous industry, development had been restricted primarily by lack of Indian capital and enterprise. Furthermore, the Congress attitude to industrial reform, for example, showed that its members were no friends of the workers.

The coming together of the educated classes, deprived of higher posts in the Civil Service, and of the businessmen who regarded themselves as discriminated against economically, was of profound importance in the struggle for freedom. It brought much-needed funds, as well as adding a further pressure in favour of non-violent reforms rather than bloody revolution, for Indian businessmen also brought the innate conservatism characteristic of capitalists of all races.

This upper middle-class minority which, in the early days of the freedom movement (1886) numbered about 300,000 in a population of 180,000,000, saw representative institutions as the only possible system which might satisfy its demands. It was not concerned with whether the British government was morally good or bad, but only with the fact that it was there, depriving educated Indians of their rightful jobs and profits.

Congress continued to represent this section of Indian society. Religious nationalism, on the other hand, was to have its appeal to the growing, partly Westernized, lower middle class. It was on these people that Westernization had a destructive effect. Being inadequately educated in an alien cultural tradition, they found themselves uneasy in their own. They became afraid of Western-style changes and saw no advantage for themselves in representative government, which they anticipated would favour the fully Westernized upper middle classes rather than themselves.

The period up to 1905 was essentially one of frustration. Congress appeared to be getting nowhere with its gradualist demands. Religious nationalism was spreading its influence but was hardly in a position to challenge the government by force. Muslims, who had been advised by Syed Ahmed to keep out of politics, did not seem to be gaining anything by their loyalty to the British. The situation was ripe for the acceptance of another European institution—the secret society. The major influences were the Carbonari of Italy and the Irish Sinn Fein. The appeal of such societies was mainly romantic, for

even such revivalist leaders as Tilak did not approve of terrorism or accept that it could lead to Indian freedom. Tilak
believed in mass agitation, not in the isolated murder of British
officials. Terrorism, indeed, was to remain only a tributary
stream in the current of Indian nationalism. But the deeds of
terrorists were followed avidly by young and old, and the idea
of liberating India by force remained the hope of some
nationalists right to the end of British rule.

Under the pressures of extremism, the fortunes of the
moderate leaders of Congress suffered continuous decline.
Their loyal and peaceful agitation was regularly rebuffed by the
British. The moderate leaders, however, were men of very real
quality. Their tragedies were the depth of their Westernization
and their trust in British good faith. (Not that this prevented
them from criticizing British rule in India.) Dadabhai Naoroji
(1825–1917), for example, a Parsee who was president of
Congress in 1886, 1893 and 1906, lived for some time in
England and had the distinction of being elected to the House
of Commons in 1892 on a Liberal ticket. His aim was to
convince the British, and particularly the legislators in Britain
itself, that they should grant liberal institutions in India.
Mahadev Govind Ranade (1842–1901), who was a judge for
thirty years and barred by his position from political activity,
concentrated on social and economic reform, and his activities
persuaded others who were politically active that such reforms
could not be divorced from political action. Gopal Krishna
Gokhale (1866–1915) believed implicitly in gradualist reform
and in co-operation rather than revolution. In 1905, Gokhale
founded the Servants of India Society. 'Its members', he said,
'frankly accept the British connection, as ordained, in the
inscrutable dispensation of Providence, for India's good. Self-
government on the lines of English colonies is their goal. This
goal, they recognise, cannot be attained without years of
earnest and patient work and sacrifices worthy of the cause.'
These men all believed in service and in the working out of

British rule—through education and the assimilation of ideas, to self-government.

They were, however, engulfed by frustration, a reaction to their fundamental ineffectiveness. The British might have responded to them—and if they had, the history of India in the twentieth century would have been different. But they did not. The concessions asked for quietly and temperately by the moderates were given to others, and under duress.

In 1905, the divorce of the moderate leaders from the trend of the times had become almost absolute. Their reasonable demands impressed neither the government nor other nationalist bodies. In the emotional excitement of Hindu revivalism, secret societies and growing economic frustration, their ideas appeared spiritless and futile.

For the very best of administrative reasons, the British decided to divide the vast province of Bengal in 1905. This move appealed to the government on grounds other than purely administrative ones. The viceroy, Lord Curzon, who viewed the matter purely in terms of efficiency, did not consider Indian responses important, primarily because he did not believe that Indian nationalism posed any real danger to the British. Others, less Olympian, thought otherwise. The lieutenant-governor of Bengal believed partition would be a blow to Bengali nationalists. He was right, and when partition was announced extremist agitators realized that here was a situation which could be emotionally exploited. Extremists began agitation, and the moderates, fearful of being left behind, joined in. Here at least was a great and specific issue which could give unity of purpose to all sections of the nationalist movement.

Two weapons were to be used in the campaign, terrorism and the economic boycott. The boycott began in August 1904. It was widely supported, especially by Indian mill-owners, and the wearing of homespun cloth became one of the manifestations of the struggle for freedom. Secret societies were formed among students; bomb-throwers and political assassins became popular heroes and their funerals scenes of hysterical emotion. A number of murders occurred, the first in Muzaffapur in 1908. For his comments in the *Kesari*, Tilak, who had been active again after his release from jail, was sentenced to six years' imprisonment on a charge of incitement to murder.

Terrorist activity was not confined to India. In 1909, Sir Curzon Wyllie was murdered by a Punjabi at the Imperial Institute in London. This at least brought home to the British public the existence of a nationalist movement in India.

Extremist ideas had, in fact, captured Congress. At the meeting at Benares in 1905, Tilak's slogan, openly opposed to the moderates and their appeals for concessions, was 'militancy—not medicancy'. But the extremists were unable to take over actual control of Congress, partly because of Dadabhai Naoroji, who was brought in for the 1906 meeting to effect a compromise. The moderate leaders in Congress officially accepted most of the extremists' ideas but expressed them in rather gentler terms. In 1907, compromise was spurned, and the extremist leaders were expelled from Congress.

Extremist activities were slowly eroded. Without Congress there was no organization. The government was as oppressive as ever. In 1911 the emotional fire of partition was doused by the reunification of Bengal. But extremism was by no means dead. It had gone underground into the hearts of the young who now clearly saw Congress for what it was, a pressure group for a minority. There had also been the sinister by-product of communalism. The agitation in Bengal had been almost entirely the work of Hindus. The Muslims had gained through partition a new province with a largely Muslim population and the campaign for reunification seemed yet another example of the Hindu majority determined to dominate all. In 1906, conservative Muslims founded the Muslim League.

The war that broke out in Europe in August 1914 brought about a truce in nationalist agitation against the British; there was in fact an outburst of enthusiasm which seems today, in the light of subsequent events, almost incomprehensible. But many nationalists thought that helping the British would result in a victory which might bring some tangible reward. This belief was encouraged by the allied statesmen's insistence that the war was being fought to make the world safe for democracy, and self-determination for all peoples was the battle cry; unfortunately, the Indian nationalists were naïve enough to believe this applied to them. At that time, nationalist opinion was directed towards achieving self-government within the British Empire and this, they thought, was comparatively little to ask. Recruits flocked to the army—some 1,200,000 volunteered—and there were spontaneous contributions to war loans and the like. The British reduced their garrison in India to 15,000 men, and many British administrators going off to fight handed their jobs to Indian subordinates. In this way, two of the nationalist demands—the reduction of the 'army of occupation' and more, higher posts for Indians—were unintentionally granted. But, like everyone else, Indians believed the war would soon be over and, when it dragged on, popular enthusiasm waned.

A change came over Congress. In 1914 it had loyally declared its support for the war in Europe. But in the following year, three of the most influential moderate leaders, including Gokhale, died and the extremists began to return. In 1916, moderates and extremists united, and in the same year Congress and the Muslim League joined together in a demand, not for independence, but for self-government within the Empire.

In the light of history it is ironic that the Congress meeting which led to a display of Hindu–Muslim concord also saw the triumph of the extremists. In 1916, Tilak and Annie Besant, in an endeavour to break the immobility of political life, had independently founded Home Rule Leagues. Though the movement had the appearance of revolutionary vigour, it was essentially conservative. Tilak's experience of British repression, which by 1914 had given him six years in jail, had turned him towards caution. Mrs Besant's aim in entering Indian politics had been primarily to bring India and Britain together, a reflection of the Eurasian nature of her religious beliefs. She was against violence and had even denounced Tilak's advocacy of passive resistance. But now she believed that Tilak had had a change of heart and her purpose was to unite in Congress all shades of nationalist opinion so that together they might engage in agitation. As she conceived it, agitation would not be violent or terroristic. Such methods would only invite the full weight of British power to crush it. Mrs Besant had in mind the classic British campaigns for reform—for the abolition of slavery, the repeal of the Corn Laws, and for Irish Home Rule. Monster public meetings, newspaper articles and pamphlets would produce widespread support and such agitation would compel the British to grant self-government. 'British politicians', she maintained, 'judge the value of claims by the energy of those who put them forward.' Only in the dull climate of political India in the middle of a war would such thoughts have been considered revolutionary.

Yet they were. The younger nationalists, frustrated by efficient government suppression, were inspired by the new call for action. Tilak, who disliked Mrs Besant, set up his own Home Rule League in Maharashtra in order to get ahead of her. For her own organization she relied on the branches of the Theosophical Society which produced the initial cadres. But many others responded to this rather faint light in the general gloom. One was Jawaharlal Nehru, already acquainted with Mrs Besant and perhaps even emotionally drawn to this surprisingly dynamic and vigorous woman of sixty-nine who had played a not inconsiderable role in his early life. In June, the government of Madras interned her and six days later a branch of the league was formed in Allahabad with Jawaharlal Nehru as its secretary.

At the Congress session of December 1917, Mrs Besant was

swept into the office of president. But once there she seemed to express a view not far from that of the moderates. It looked as if she was advocating caution and had decided to await the outcome of new reforms which were foreshadowed in August of that year by the announcement that new advances were to be made towards responsible government in India. At the session of 1918, Mrs Besant's leadership was rejected by the young men of Congress as well as by the extremists. But she had succeeded in changing the whole character of the organization. The moderates began to leave the movement they had dominated for so long with their constitutional approach to change. The overwhelming majority of Congress members by 1919 were young men and extremists. Even the offer of new reforms had been basically a response to the fact that the British government in London had realized that its failure to answer the demands of the moderates had driven them to support the home-rulers.

Mrs Besant's legacy to the new Congress which discarded her was an all-India organization and an agitational style. Tilak had foreshadowed it, so had the extremists in the Punjab and in Bengal, but the home-rule activity of the years 1915–18 had aroused a wide range of interests to a sense of solidarity and shared impatience. It was upon this basis that a new leader, Mahatma Gandhi, was to build a new sort of national movement, in which envy and frustration were apparently sublimated into the total rejection of British rule.

VISIONS OF THE WEST

'The departure of the wise men from the East', remarked the English wit Sydney Smith in 1835, 'seems to have been on a more extensive scale than is generally supposed, for no one of that description seems to have been left behind.' In the same year, Thomas Babington Macaulay, then law member of the government of British India, dismissed Hindu civilization because it tolerated 'medical doctrines which would disgrace an English farrier, Astronomy, which would move laughter in girls at an English boarding school, History abounding with kings thirty feet high, and reigns thirty thousand years long, and Geography, made up of seas of treacle and seas of butter'. The authentic tones of Western cultural arrogance were not at first resented by the emerging Indian intelligentsia. They surveyed their apparently decaying civilization, recognized its fragility in the face of the dynamism of the conqueror, and looked avidly for the secret of the West's success. The Mystic East was parallelled by the Mysterious Occident; exoticism became a two-way street.

Educated Indians thought the secret of British superiority might lie in their religion. Coming from a society in which every aspect was validated and sustained by religion, it was the obvious thing to think. At an early stage, Christianity and Western-style education were so closely linked that many young Hindus became convinced that they could not have one without the other. This posed the threat of conversion, though the number of converts to Christianity among the educated classes was comparatively small, and remained so, in part because most converts in India came from the lower castes seeking a higher social position and better economic opportunities by adopting the religion of the rulers.

The ethical ideas of Christianity, however, did have their appeal, and a number of attempts were made to absorb these—and in particular the humanitarian elements—without actual conversion. This led to movements whose principal aim was the reform and modernization of Hinduism, to maintain its validity but to introduce changes in its social expression so that it could be more responsive to modern needs.

The first of the modernizers, that protean figure, Ram Mohun Roy, sought to demonstrate that the humanitarian ideas of Western Christianity were already present in Hinduism, though they had become overlaid by superstition and corruption. He attacked Hindu idolatry as a later accretion to the simple and basically monotheistic concepts of the classical Hindu scriptures. Ram Mohun was, in fact, the first of the cultural and religious nationalists to see—though without rancour or racial arrogance—the humanitarian concepts of Western liberalism (even, indeed, the seeds of Western science) in Hindu civilization. Replying to an attack made on him by Christian missionaries because he rejected the divinity of Jesus, Ram Mohun states his viewpoint.

If by the 'ray of intelligence' for which the Christian says we are indebted to the English, he means the introduction of useful mechanical arts, I am ready to express my assent and also my gratitude; but with respect to *science, literature,* or *religion*, I do not acknowledge that we are placed under any obligation. For by a reference to History it may be proved that the world was indebted to *our ancestors* for the first dawn of knowledge, which sprang up in the East, and thanks to the Goddess of Wisdom, we have still a philosophical and copious language of our own which distinguishes us from other nations who cannot express scientific or abstract ideas without borrowing the language of foreigners.

[158]

Nevertheless, Ram Mohun believed that India could benefit from Western ideas and was a firm supporter of English education. There was no hesitation, on his part, about accepting anything the British had to offer that was not present at a similar level of sophistication in Hindu society. This did not, however, entail accepting the ideological basis of Western society as well.

Unlike Ram Mohun Roy, whose aim was to restate the dignity of the Hindu world, Henry Derozio (1809–31) sought to identify as completely as possible with the West.

Derozio was a Eurasian who had been reared as a Protestant Christian. When he was seventeen, he wrote some romantic poems which made him the talk of intellectual Calcutta, and two years later he became assistant headmaster of the Hindu College. There, his expression in Indian terms of the patriotic sentiments and aspirations of his poetic masters—the English romantics, Byron and Shelley—gave him tremendous influence over the minds of young Bengalis.

Under Derozio's influence, Bengali middle-class youth studied Francis Bacon, Hume and Tom Paine. Paine's *Age of Reason*, a hundred copies of which had been advertised for sale by a Calcutta bookseller, was soon the subject of a flourishing black market and copies were changing hands at five times the original price. Part of the book was later reprinted in a Bengali-language magazine.

In 1828, Derozio founded the Academic Association for discussion of advanced social and political ideas. The subjects considered included 'free will, free ordination, fate, faith, the sacredness of truth, the high duty of cultivating virtue, the meanness of vice, the nobility of patriotism, the attributes of God, and the arguments for and against the existence of the Deity as these have been set forth by Hume on the one side, and Reid, Dugald Stewart and Brown on the other, the hollowness of idolatry and the shams of the priesthood'.

The numbers of students who had access to and discussed

Western social and political ideas were extremely small. In 1828, there were only 436 students on the rolls of the Hindu College—but they formed a seminal minority. They were almost entirely Western in their outlook, so much so that the Calcutta newspaper, *The Englishman*, reported in May 1836 of former students of the Hindu College that

> in matters of politics, they are all radicals, and are followers of Benthamite principles. The very word Tory is a sort of ignominy among them. They think that toleration ought to be practised by every government, and the best and surest way of making the people abandon their barbarous customs and rites is by diffusing education among them. With respect to the questions relating to Political Economy, they all belong to the school of Adam Smith. They are clearly of opinion that the system of monopoly, the restraints upon trade, and the international laws of many countries, do nothing but paralyse the efforts of the industry, impede the progress of agriculture and manufacture and prevent commerce from flowing in its natural course.

The students of Hindu College published a number of magazines, most of them concerned with political, social and scientific matters. The views they expressed were far in advance of those of Ram Mohun Roy, who was not infrequently attacked in their pages. One of Ram Mohun's projects was that a colony of Englishmen should be established in India. This idea was ridiculed in a paper given at a meeting of the Hindu Literary Society. 'No sooner did the benevolent inhabitants of Europe behold the sad condition of the natives', the author of the paper remarked, 'than they immediately got to work to ameliorate and improve it. They introduced among them, *rum*, *gin*, *brandy* and the other comforts of life, and it is astonishing to read how soon the poor savages learnt to estimate these *blessings*.'

Some Indians at least had learned quite early the difference between literature and reality, the gap between what they now had access to, through their knowledge of the English language, ideas of liberty, equality, and parliamentary democracy which the British had fought for and now took for granted in Britain, and the distinctly unequal and authoritarian government imposed upon them by the same British in India.

The value placed upon British political processes and institutions was, in the estimation of the Indian educated-classes, only enhanced by the refusal of the British to grant them to their colonial subjects! British political philosophies and practices were not the only ones made available to Indians by way of their knowledge of English. A whole new world of European thought—though one restricted by the filter of English translation and commentary—was also opened up: the ideas of the French Revolution of 1789 and its successors, of the Italian *risorgimento*, of anarchism, and communism.

Such discoveries were, of course, not made overnight. They took time to penetrate even the small minority of educated Indians. But in the second half of the nineteenth century two strands of Western political thought, the evolutionary and the revolutionary, were securely woven into the attitudes of the politicized classes. Moderates retained a belief in the evolutionary processes of parliamentary democracy. Some professed a Gladstonian liberalism, others were impressed by the lives and ideas of Garibaldi, Mazzini and Cavour. But whatever their models, all the moderates believed in equality of political rights. But there were others who rejected the revolutionary concept of equality, so alien to the structure of Hindu society which is based on the acknowledged inequality between castes. This reaction produced extremist movements, but these were more than just an atavistic reaction to Western ideas. The history of the West had shown that the most important political unit was the nation-state and the strength of the nation lay in its sense of folk, community and history.

Before the coming of European cultural historians, most Indians had known little of their own past. They were unable to observe the historical process, because they were unaware of its existence. European curiosity dug up India's past, its literature, its religions and its heroes, and in doing so gave to Indians a living sense of historical reality.

In the latter part of the nineteenth century, the Western-educated unemployed discovered their Hindu past, presented to them by European scholars. Their reaction to this unexpected inheritance was a blending of Western ideas of nationalism with enthusiasm for the old religion, of Western techniques of political agitation with *revenants* from the Hindu past. Revolution was their aim, not slow progress towards the Western democratic ideal. The vocabulary of their revolution was purely Western. The precedent of the French Revolution was widely quoted. So, too, was Garibaldi. Secret societies were formed, some of them modelled upon the Italian Carbonari or the Irish Sinn Fein. The violent doctrines of the Hungarian revolutionary Louis Kossuth (1802–94) were eagerly received. The concept of a war of independence was taken from the United States; from Ireland, the weapon of the boycott; from Russia, the secret organization of the Nihilists.

But the ideology was strictly Hindu. The *Bhagavad-gita* became a devotional manual and its teaching was perverted to give sanction to assassination. The goddess Kali, the destroyer of demons, became the Joan of Arc of Bengali nationalists. They rearmed her with the bomb and the pistol, the classic weapons of European rebellion.

Religious terrorism was repugnant to those moderate Indians who pinned their faith on the evolutionary process and the promises of the British. So, too, in the twentieth century, their heirs were repelled by the non-violent religious terrorism of Mahatma Gandhi. Most of the believers in Western-style Westminster democracy were hurled aside by the atavistic flood, though their slogans were displayed by Congress in

order to present a modern face sufficiently appealing to demo-
crats and anti-colonialists in Britain and America, to ensure
their continuing interest and support.

During the period of almost frenetic reform between 1820
and 1850, the British introduced legislation abolishing slavery,
female infanticide and widow-burning, and suppressed
Thugee, a religiously authenticated banditry. After these great
and rather dramatic social reforms, the British felt thay had
interfered enough. There were Westernized Indians, however,
who were convinced that the government should go further.
One area ripe for reform was that of female education. Before
1858, the government of India was not willing to provide
education for women. In response both to missionary pressure
and to the infiltration of general ideas of Western liberalism, a
certain amount of agitation did, however, grow up over the
status of women in general and widows in particular. A number
of Indians proposed legislation to raise the minimum marriage
age, and to permit the remarriage of Hindu widows. Although
the government preferred not to initiate legislation itself, and
generally resisted attempts to pressurize it into enacting legislation which it believed would interfere in religious matters, it
allowed itself to be persuaded by Isvarchandra Vidyasagar to
pass the Hindu Widows Remarriage Act of 1856.

Hindu polygamy was another matter which brought many
petitions to the government between 1855 and 1857. In 1855,
the Maharaja of Burdwan described the evils he believed
should be legislated against. The particular offenders were a
Brahmin caste in Bengal known as Kulins.

Those Koolins, who cannot get persons of equal caste
willing to effect matrimonial alliances with them, nor afford
the large marriage gratuities which are demanded, are
obliged to let their daughters arrive at old age without being
married. Koolin Brahmins never marry without receiving
large donations and multiply wives for the sake of obtaining

[163]

these gratuities without knowing or caring what becomes of the women to whom they are united by the most solemn rites of their religion. They have been known to marry more than a hundred wives each; and it is customary with them, immediately after going through the nuptial ceremony and receiving their gratuities, to leave the houses of the girls they have married, never to see their faces more.

Legislation was drafted, but the outbreak of the Mutiny held up proceedings, and when the lieutenant-governor of Bengal later asked the government of India to enact legislation it refused, on the grounds that it might set a precedent which might not be approved by others practising polygamy (principally Muslims) outside Bengal.

In the second half of the nineteenth century, the real incentive came from Indian reformers who regarded female education as part of their general campaign to raise the status of women. One of the most influential of these was a Brahmin widow who had been converted to Christianity, Pandita Ramabhai (1858–1922). At Poona in the Bombay presidency she built a home for Hindu widows which was also a centre of Sanskrit learning. The Western conception of equality for women was implicit in Ramabhai's ideas and her views on education were dedicated to the same premise. Naturally, her activities aroused considerable opposition, but her home at Poona flourished—at one time there were as many as 2,000 Hindu widows there.

The movement towards extension of education for both Hindu and Muslim women undoubtedly owed its principal impetus to the nationalist movement. Egalitarian political ideas had some effect on the social position of women and, generally speaking, nationalists were in favour of female education. Nevertheless, the number of girls at school increased very slowly. In the field of higher education, however, the picture was more satisfactory. In 1935, for example, about 5,000 women were studying for university degrees. In 1892, there had been only eighty-six, and even as late as 1929 only 1,800. But the educational standard of the candidates left much to be desired. Of the 5,000 students of 1935, only 460 actually graduated. These figures are not unsatisfactory when they are compared with those for men students.

The absorption, by a sort of osmosis, of Victorian moral values not infrequently brought educated Indians and the British in India together in an alliance of unconscious stupidity. Ideas of temperance and social purity appealed to many politicized Indians. Mahatma Gandhi was by no means the first to recognize a parallel between such ideas and the ascetic tradition of Hinduism, in which self-denial, vegetarianism and sexual abstention are considered valuable aids to spiritual development.

The National Social Conference, founded in 1887, met after the annual sessions of Congress and continually passed resolutions on social purity. These resolutions often led to active campaigns. In Madras, one R. V. R. Naidu, a school headmaster, was a prominent figure in such campaigns. He heartily condemned masturbation, 'That hideous sin engendered by vice and practised in solitude', 'indecent pictures', impure thoughts and—nautch dances.

During most of the nineteenth century an extravagant form of entertainment was to provide a nautch, a sort of Indian ballet, for one's guests. The providers of such entertainment were often persons of standing and consequence, and their guests members of the British ruling elite. When Edward, Prince of Wales, toured India in 1875, he was entertained at a nautch. So was his eldest son, the Duke of Clarence, fifteen years later. There were no complaints at the time of the visit of the heir to the throne, but in 1890, a memorial was forwarded by the Bishop of Calcutta to the viceroy, alleging that such performances had an 'immoral character'. The viceroy replied that he considered the whole business 'perfectly decorous'.

If the viceroy hoped to get away with a simple rebuttal, he was mistaken. The missionary press, and in particular, the *Sentinel*, a weekly journal that criticized such things as drinking, smoking and vivisection, as well as arms manufacture and imperialism, described the nautch as being 'performed by Hindu prostitutes, who usually sing songs of the most lascivious character, accompanied by gestures and movements of the body having an obscene meaning'. How the viceroy had missed such overt eroticism, the author could not understand.

Concerned Indians, including Naidu and Subramaniya Aiyer, editor of the Madras English-language daily, the *Hindu*, who was so 'advanced' as to be disowned by orthodox Hindus, produced memorials and petitions. One such inspired a response from the governor of Madras, who could not see how one could follow such puritanical principles in England; 'we shall not be able to attend any theatrical performances till we have satisfied ourselves as to the moral character of the performers'. The English-owned newspaper, the *Madras Mail*, however, called for British support for the anti-nautch campaign, and justified its attitude by asserting that 'the Hindu social reformer is the product of our Western education, and he must not be left to struggle on alone.'

The attitude of the official elite was one of indifference but the campaign continued. The redoubtable R. V. R. Naidu introduced a resolution at the Congress session of 1894, conveniently held at Madras, condemning nautches. In his speech in support of the proposition, Naidu suggested that once the immorality of Indian dancing had been purged, there would be an aesthetic regeneration. He was to be proved wrong. When the future king-emperor, George V, and his wife visited Madras in 1906, it was decided that the couple would not be entertained at a nautch. Instead they were offered 'Hindustani music', 'Herculean feats by Ramamurti' (a famous gymnast), and 'Magic and Conjuring by Professor Swaminatha

Sastriar', a programme which turned out to be both trivial and boring, though certainly moral.

Some Indians—if they could afford it—transmuted their visions of the West into a local reality by creating a physical and mental environment totally alien to that of the vast majority of their compatriots. They lived, as far as possible, in the European manner, wearing European clothes, building and decorating their homes in the current European taste, eating meat, drinking French wines, London gin and Scotch whisky. But others sought a compromise between imitation and revivalism, and, incidentally, a very British sort of compromise—the 'happy medium'. One such was Motilal Nehru.

Early in the eighteenth century, Motilal Nehru's ancestor, a distinguished Sanskrit and Persian scholar named Raj Kaul, left his home in Kashmir for the Mughal imperial capital of Delhi. He was very much following the tradition for men of his caste and country, for he was Brahmin, a man of the elite in the Hindu social order. Kashmiri Brahmins, men of both learning and ambition but no great wealth, had for centuries left their mountainous but economically arid homeland to occupy places of authority and trust in the administration of the Mughal Empire and in that of the Hindu princes in alliance with it. They made up a small community, very conscious of the ties of kinship and of their superiority of learning. Their pride was only matched by the handsomeness of their men and the beauty of their women. Like the Scots, away from their birthplace they were ever mourning their exile.

Raj Kaul, however, even though he had been invited to Delhi by the Mughal emperor himself, had chosen a time when the imperial patronage was weakening. Yet Raj Kaul would hardly have noticed it. In the usual manner he was given a grant of land, with a house situated by a canal on the outskirts of Delhi. From this location and to differentiate him from the other Kauls, he added 'Nehru' from the Urdu word for a canal, *nahar*, and for some years the family was known as Kaul-Nehru.

Despite the vicissitudes of the imperial house, as long as it reigned—though by the middle of the century it no longer effectively *ruled*—a Kaul-Nehru occupied some official position. But not always with the Mughals. One Lakshmi Narayan Nehru (by this time the family had dropped the 'Kaul'), perhaps sensing a change in the wind, became the first *vakil*, a sort of combination of legal adviser and representative of the English East India Company, at the court of the virtually powerless Mughal emperor.

The Mutiny of 1857 ended the Nehrus' connection with Delhi. Pandit Ganga Dhar Nehru had been the chief of police in the city before the terrible events that led to the final extinction of the Mughals. After the collapse of the revolt, the Nehrus left Delhi for Agra, once the second city of Mughal India but by then somewhat tattered. Even the glorious marble monument of the Taj Mahal had been turned into an armoury. Early in 1861 Ganga Dhar died. A few months later, on 6 May, his son Motilal was born.

With his father dead, Motilal became the responsibility of his elder brothers. One was in government service, the other, Nandlal, after a period in the employ of a petty raja, qualified in law and began to practise at the Agra Bar. It was upon Nandlal that the active responsibility for Motilal's upbringing was placed, and when the High Court was moved from Agra to Allahabad, the Nehru family also moved to this quiet provincial town.

For the first twelve years of his life, Motilal was educated at home. His lessons were mainly in Arabic and Persian, the languages and the literature of the once-ruling Muslims. This might seem an eccentric cultural emphasis for a Brahmin, the highest of the Hindu castes in a part of India that is so much the heartland of Hinduism. The United Provinces of Agra and Oudh (now the state of Uttar Pradesh) not only contains the junction of the sacred rivers at Allahabad, then the provincial capital, but also the mecca of Hinduism, Benares. To the north are the Himalayas, where on Mount Kailas dwells Shiva, the most important of the gods. At Ayodhya was the capital of the hero of the *Ramayana*, Rama the golden king of a golden age. And the area around Mathura had been the scene of many of the escapades of that most popular of Hindu deities, the divine cowherd Krishna.

The nearness of gods and heroes had preserved Hindu values from the threats of a succession of non-Hindu conquerors. The mass of the population remained faithful to their tradition, but it did not command the allegiance of the elite. They became steeped in a culture whose inspiration was Muslim. Some of the Hindu elite also took the religion of the Muslim conquerors, but many Brahmins and members of the influentially placed writer-caste, the *kayasthas*, while remaining Hindus adopted much of the Islamized culture. Among the smaller groups who accepted this Indo-Persian culture were the Kashmiri Pandits. The position of members of these groups, men in effect of two cultures, reflected their relationship with the Muslim rulers. That relationship was one of service, of intimacy but not identification with whatever government was in power. With the coming of the British, these groups welcomed the opportunities they offered for Western-style education. They found service in the administration as they had done before, or took employment with those elements such as the large landlords whose position had been enhanced by British rule. Many retained their two-culture allegiance to which they added another, that of the West.

Motilal Nehru followed such a course. From private tuition in Arabic and Persian, he moved to an English education at the Government High School at Cawnpore (Kanpur) and the Muir Central College, Allahabad. There he acquired a deep admiration for Western ideas and also for the Western manner of life. But Motilal did not take his degree. Doing, as he thought, badly in the first paper of his BA examination, he stayed away from the rest. On the surface it was a foolish decision, for at this time a university degree was the only passport to a well-paid job in government employ. Fortunately, this moment of weakness passed, and turning to the study of law, Motilal took his examinations, topping the list of successful candidates. In 1883 he went to serve his apprenticeship at Cawnpore and three years later returned to Allahabad to begin practice at the High Court.

No sooner had Motilal begun to establish himself at Allahabad than tragedy struck the Nehru family. Nandlal, who had built up a lucrative practice, died in 1887 at the age of forty-two, leaving a widow, two daughters and five sons. Motilal now found himself the head and sole support of a large family. He was twenty-six years old. He himself was married but had no children. It was Motilal's second marriage. There had been a child of his first, but both mother and child had died. For Motilal the tragedy was not yet over, for a boy born to his second wife was also to die in infancy. Under the circumstances it is hardly surprising that when a second son was born on 14 November 1889 his arrival was an occasion for particular rejoicing.

For the first three years of the boy Jawaharlal's life, the family lived deep in the city, not far from the central market. But the direction of Motilal's life was towards great financial rewards and increasing Westernization in his style of living. The family moved to a bungalow in what were known as the Civil Lines, a residential area mainly for Europeans, reflecting both their aloofness from the India of the crowded city and their desire to show their superiority to it. Even though the bungalow on Elgin Road was not particularly luxurious compared with some of the mansions of the British which surrounded it, the move was significant. Motilal Nehru's choice was not just that of a man earning large sums of money who moves into a better house in a more fashionable district. Though the Civil Lines and the city were only separated by a few hundred yards, mentally and socially they were worlds apart. Motilal Nehru was following the tradition of his community and attaching himself to the values of the conqueror.

But not to the exclusion of all others. Motilal's wife, Swarup Rani, remained a Hindu wife with little interest in anything but her home and her family. Motilal himself did not reject tradition. The atmosphere in the Nehru home, however, was more English than Indian, and increasingly so as Motilal's earnings at the Bar rose higher and higher. In 1900 Motilal purchased a large house with extensive grounds in Church Road and named it Anand Bhawan—Abode of Happiness. A great deal of money was spent on making it a palatial home.

Anand Bhawan symbolized the cultures which had come to dominate the lives of the Nehrus. The house itself was Indian in style: a big, rambling house with large rooms and many terraces, which gave the impression of great height. The rooms were built around a courtyard with a fountain in the centre. There was also a swimming pool and the house was the first in Allahabad to have electricity and piped water. Motilal, like his son later, was attracted by science. But Motilal's interest was mainly in the practical. In this sense he was very much the Victorian polymath. Among the law books and the English classics in his library were manuals on such subjects as *Practical Bell-fitting* and a detailed work, *A Practical Treatise upon the Fitting of Hot-Water Apparatus*.

Still, the house was divided between the Indian and the Western. In the Indian part, the women and children lived a comfortable but essentially traditional life. The kitchens were in the charge of Brahmin cooks and the servants were all Hindus. On the first days of every month, large quantities of rice were cleaned and wheat ground in stone hand mills on the kitchen floor. In the Western part, there were cooks and servants who had been trained to work in English homes; Goans or Mughs from Bengal were in charge of the kitchens, while the other servants were Muslims, for no Hindu would handle meat. Motilal ate in the Western dining-room, sitting on a chair at table. Most of the family ate in the Indian dining-room, sitting on mats upon the marble floor. To point the ambivalence, Motilal always wore European clothes out-side the house but the traditional kurta and pyjamas of the province—wide trousers and knee-length shirt of fine muslin —inside. For ceremonial occasions he would wear a long black or white coat—the *achkan* which his son was to make famous throughout the world—and close-fitting, almost legging-like trousers.

This catholicity of behaviour embraced religious festivals. The Hindu calendar abounds with them. All were observed. But so was the Muslim *Nowroz*, the celebration of the New Year, which in Kashmir was as much a Hindu festival as a Muslim one. Members of the family would also join Muslim friends to eat sweet vermicelli scented with rose water and decorated with gold and silver leaf at the end of the fast of *Ramadan*. Christmas, it seems, was not observed in Anand Bhawan, but the children were allowed to go to parties given by their Christian friends and baskets of flowers were sent to decorate the church of the Holy Trinity which stood next door. Anand Bhawan itself occupied sacred ground, for according to legend the hero Rama had been greeted by his brother Bharat at the end of his long exile at a spot in the garden. Every year, that meeting was celebrated by a procession which ended at Anand Bhawan.

Motilal tried to arrange for his son a Eurasian education: English tutors for the sort of schooling an English boy of his class might receive, and learned Brahmins to teach him Hindi and Sanskrit. The last did not have much, if any, success. The first introduced the boy to Lewis Carroll, and to Rudyard Kipling, whose *Jungle Books* and *Kim* were great favourites. There were Scott and Dickens and Thackeray, the romances of H. G. Wells and tales of real-life explorers, as well as the better known English poets. Later Motilal decided upon an authentic English education in England. He sent his son to

Harrow, and then to Cambridge University. After graduation, the idea that young Nehru might sit the entry examination for the Indian Civil Service was abandoned, though not for any political reason, and instead he read for the English Bar.

Politically, Motilal was a moderate, a constitutionalist. He first attended a meeting of Congress in 1888, which was held that year in Allahabad. It was more of a social than a political act, a gesture of identification with men of his own kind, and after 1892 his name disappears from the lists of delegates. Motilal was too busy building up a law practice to give time to active politics. But he was not out of touch. There was, indeed, every reason why he should not be. Congress was the trade union of his class—the Westernized bourgeoisie. Among its leaders, Motilal particularly admired G. K. Gokhale, highly Westernized, a constitutionalist by conviction, and a loyalist of principle, who was to say that if the British were to leave India, Indians would call them back before they reached Aden! Gokhale reconciled, as did Motilal and others like him, genuine Indian patriotism with loyalty to Britain.

In 1905, Motilal returned to Congress, to help defend moderation against the extremists. His son favoured the extremist point of view, but both shared a firm belief in British justice, that apotheosis of 'fair play', and in liberal realism. Father and son were to have their beliefs shattered by the massacre at the Jallianwala Bagh, in the Punjab city of Amritsar in April 1919. In this apparent display of institutional violence by the British, the Nehrus discerned for the first time the dark face of the civilization which had moulded their lives and thoughts. It also brought them into contact with Mahatma Gandhi.

The effect of the Mahatma on the elder Nehru was, again, something of a compromise. Motilal accepted a more personal identification with his fellow-countrymen, by abandoning his European style of dress, his elegant suits and collars and cravats, in favour of homespun ethnic garments. Also put aside

[173]

was the luxury of his household. Austerity was to reign at Anand Bhawan, though it was not by any stretch of the imagination the austerity of the ashram, the holy poverty of the Mahatma. But non-cooperation was another matter. In 1920 Motilal seemed ready to support non-cooperation, and in 1922 he and his son found themselves in a British jail for agitating in its favour. But in the next year, Motilal returned to his old belief in constitutional progress. He and others who questioned the Mahatma's rejectionist leadership formed a new political organization, the *Swaraj* or Freedom Party, to fight new elections under an expanded franchise which had been granted by the British, partly because of the non-cooperation campaign.

The party did rather well in the elections, and set about disrupting the work of the legislatures as an expression of popular sentiment. As the government retained powers to push through legislation, this form of non-cooperation hardly affected the administration. But it did demonstrate, as the Swaraj leaders had intended, a show of strength as well as a warning that constitutional reforms, insufficiently progressive, might always be nullified by the use of the democratic vote. The Mahatma and Motilal's son rejected this premise. For them, the legislatures should be boycotted. The function of Congress, they insisted, was to return to the grass-roots, not to give credibility to British institutions by trying to destroy them from inside.

Late in 1926, the Mahatma's view triumphed. The Swaraj Party walked out of the legislature as many of its members had succumbed to the temptation to take office. It was to be over a decade later, and with Motilal dead, that the temptations were to be renewed and were so seductive with the possibilities of real power that even the Mahatma approved Congress falling for them.

The belief in the virtues of the best of the West played a significant and basically healthy role in Indian nationalism.

Both the Nehrus, Motilal, who died in 1930, and his son, Jawaharlal, who, seventeen years later became the first prime minister of independent India, remained men of two worlds. Their separate and often coinciding visions of the West saved them from losing themselves completely in the darkness of Gandhi's Hindu world, and in the end, to gain a partial victory over it.

Part Four

MAKING
THE MAHATMA

LAWYER

The theatre of the Mahatma's life is a theatre of masks: Lawyer, Freedom Fighter, Giant Killer. Behind lurks the figure of Mohandas Karamchand Gandhi, a much more interesting, if curiously smaller, figure. The Mahatma's life is well documented; indeed, it is almost drowned in documentation, millions of words, his own, other people's, much of it trivia, fortunately mostly unread, but nevertheless sanctified by its monumentality. However, it is still possible to discern something of the man behind the monument, something of the reality behind the myth.

In February 1948, a month after the assassination in the garden of Birla House, New Delhi, the little state of Junagadh in Kathiawar, the probable homeland of the Mahatma's family and undoubtedly that of his mother, held a plebiscite. Its purpose was to decide whether the inhabitants of this little princely state wished to become citizens of the newly independent India or of the equally new and independent Pakistan. Wisely, they voted for India.

The need for a plebiscite lay in the fact that at the time Britain granted freedom to a Raj divided into two new states, one still called India and the other Pakistan, they also gave freedom to the princely states. In one sense, the rulers, Hindu rajas and maharajas and Muslim nawabs, were faced by two choices, independence for themselves, or the acceptance of some sort of tributary relationship with the successors to the British Crown. Accession to either India or Pakistan was really their only choice—and it ought to have been one dependent simply upon geographical location. Most made the sensible decision. In the end only three of the nearly 600 principalities were to be awkward: Hyderabad, the largest; Kashmir, which is still in contention today; and Junagadh.

The trouble with Junagadh did not break out until after 15 August, 1947, the day of independence from British rule, when it became known that the Muslim nawab had decided to accede to Pakistan and that Pakistan had accepted the accession. The Nawab of Junagadh was not untypical of many of the princes. The 'eccentricity' of his tastes had been discreetly overlooked by the British in payment for the loyalty of him and his like. There were so many wicked princes in India that the record of their lives is more like an additional volume by the Brothers Grimm than a glossary of the sort of people one would expect to be allies of such a moral people as the British. But as in so many things, India provided the exceptions. The king-emperor needed tributary kings in order to enhance his glory. He got some very queer ones, and just a few who were good and reasonably decent rulers. On the whole, the preservation of the princes in the amber of British power is one of the less pleasant aspects of British rule in India. The true conditions of the states were too often concealed behind the romantic novelist's view of jewelled elephants, gorgeous turbans and 'age-old magic'. The princes encouraged this view, and got on with enjoying their 'age-old' vices.

The ruler of Junagadh was no exception. He loved to watch deliberately wounded animals torn to pieces by deliberately starved hounds. Surrounding his palace were rooms, pleasantly furnished, and each with a servant and a telephone, for every one of his hundred or so dogs. In fact, a dog's life in Junagadh was infinitely superior to that of the majority of the people. This comparatively small state of 4,000 square miles lay on the south-western coast of the Kathiawar peninsula, an area of great beauty and scenic grandeur. Its chief sea port was some 350 miles away from Karachi, the new capital of Pakistan, and it was surrounded on all sides except the sea by states which had acceded to India. The complex of states in Kathiawar was like some demented jigsaw. Most were tiny fragments scattered over the peninsula. There were even bits of Junagadh embedded as enclaves inside other states, and enclaves of other states' territories remained inside Junagadh. As late as July, the Nawab of Junagadh had given the impression that, though he himself was a Muslim, he would accede to India as most of the other states in Kathiawar had already decided to do so. It was a most sensible decision, since over 80 per cent of the 816,000 inhabitants of Junagadh were Hindu. But the nawab postponed the actual signing of the instrument of accession—and then plumped for Pakistan. He even went further and occupied two tiny states, Mangrol and Babariawad, which had decided to accede to India in an attempt to assert their independence of him and the overlordship he claimed over them.

The other Kathiawar states, led by Nawanagar, regarding this as a threat to peace, appealed to the new government of India and began to mass their own state troops on the Junagadh borders. Indian troops in Kathiawar were now reinforced to a strength of 1,400 men, a troop of light tanks, and a squadron of aircraft. In addition to these, there were 2,000 states' troops. On 26 October, seeing the red light, the nawab left Junagadh in his private aircraft, with the state jewels, as many dogs as he could get aboard, and three of his four wives, for the safety of Karachi. The chief minister, faced with disorders organized by Congress workers, soon appealed to the government of India to take over the administration of the state. The government agreed, and Indian troops crossed the state frontier.

The Mahatma does not appear to have been much concerned over the events taking place in his homeland—there were certainly more obviously pressing matters demanding his time. Yet, in the last stand of the ruler of Junagadh against the tide of history lies a paradigm of Gandhi's India: the absence of any fundamental questioning of traditional structures, the tolerance of absurd and dangerous irresponsibility, as long as it was supported by tradition; and the lack of concern with cruelty to both humans and animals.

The Kathiawar from which the ruler of Junagadh fled in his aeroplane had changed very little from the one Gandhi had been born into nearly eighty years before. It still lay on the periphery of the modern world, not actually in the Middle Ages but trying hard. Junagadh, Rajkot, Porbandar, the triangle enclosing Gandhi's ancestry, in spite of the sea, the Arabian Sea, stretching outwards to the West, remained turned in upon itself. The connection with the mainland of India was a salt plain, often under water, a *cordon salinaire*. Its principalities, a salmagundi of piddling baronies, had once been notorious for palace intrigues and local wars, but had been disciplined by the British. Local wars were prohibited; palace intrigues were not, as long as they remained inside the palace.

The people of this backwater were predominantly Hindu, though there was a sizeable Muslim minority. The two communities lived comfortably together, the outwardness of the Muslims complementing the inwardness of the Hindus in matters of trade. Hindus tried to avoid crossing the sea—the black water—for fear of pollution; Muslims looked across the sea to Mecca. Hindus wove cotton and silk cloth in their homes; the Muslims loaded them upon ships and sailed them to the ports of Arabia and eastern Africa.

Both Gandhi's parents were devotees of the god Vishnu, most widely worshipped in his eighth incarnation of Krishna, in his youth the divine cowherd whose amorous adventures are part of the popular consciousness. Krishna is also the divine charioteer of the *Bhagavad Gita*, which was to become the Mahatma's favourite text. In the Gandhi family, the discipline of faith was expressed in vows and fasts, in ritual, the commonplaces of Hinduism. These were reinforced by the extremism of the Jains, once a breakaway reform movement which had long lost its radical expression and become more rigid than the

Hinduism it hoped to reform. Jains believe that all living things, humans, animals, plants, insects, water and wind, earth and fire, have souls. Believing too in the doctrine of *karma*, of a continuing cycle of return in a status defined by one's behaviour in the previous life, Jains refrain from taking *any* life. Devout Jains will wear a mask over their mouths in case they should inhale insects; some will not wash their clothes and some prefer to go without them altogether. Jainism could be said to be non-violence taken to the ultimate.

The young Gandhi's response to his parents' beliefs was to break at least some of them. He tried eating meat—strictly taboo—with the help of a Muslim friend. Gandhi found it disgusting, though he might have thought differently if the quality of the meat and the cooking had been better. He conformed with Hindu practice and married. Both partners were about the same age: twelve. Though it was the more usual practice in child-marriages for the bride to return to her parental home after a symbolic visit to the groom's house, this was not the case this time. The marriage was consummated on the wedding night.

Four years later took place one of the best known and most consequential events of Gandhi's life. He was sixteen and his father was bed-ridden . . .

I had the duties of a nurse . . . Every night I massaged his legs and retired only when he asked me to do so or after he had fallen asleep. I loved to do this service . . . This was also the time when my wife was expecting a baby—a circumstance which, as I can see today, meant a double shame for me. For one thing I did not restrain myself as I should have done. And secondly, this carnal lust got the better of . . . my devotion to my parents . . . Every night whilst my hands were busy massaging my father's legs, my mind was hovering about the bed-room—and that too at a time when religion, medical science and common sense alike forbade sexual intercourse. I was always glad to be relieved from my duty, and went straight to the bed-room after doing obeisance to my father.

It was 10:30 or 11 p.m. I was giving the massage [to his father]. My uncle offered to relieve me. I was glad and went straight to the bedroom. My wife, poor thing, was fast asleep. But how could she sleep when I was there? I woke her up. In five or six minutes, however, the servant knocked at the door. I started with alarm. 'Get up,' he said.

'What is the matter?' . . .

'Father is no more.' . . .

I felt deeply ashamed and miserable. I ran to my father's room. I saw that, if animal passion had not blinded me, I should have been spared the torture of separation from my father during his last moments. I should have been massaging him, and he would have died in my arms . . .

The shame . . of my carnal desire even at the critical hour of my father's death . . . is a blot I have never been able to efface or forget . . . Although my devotion to my parents knew no bounds . . . it was weighed and found unpardonably wanting because my mind was at the same moment in the grip of lust.

It was not, in fact, until fifteen years later and after the birth of his fifth child that Gandhi made a serious attempt to dominate his sexual desires. He did so—though not altogether successfully—in a very Hindu way: he turned his attempt into a magical act, thereby converting an abstention into a profit. Gandhi exchanged sex for power, or thought he had. 'Ability to retain and assimilate the vital fluid [he meant semen] is a matter of long training. When properly conserved it is transmuted into matchless energy and strength.'

This statement has very ancient roots, in particular the assumption that the human sexual libido is in some way identical with the creative and beneficial energy essence of the universe. From this assumption arises another, that a serious spiritual loss, a loss of power, results from normal sexual relations with a woman, or even in erotic dreams. A popular belief of long standing in India, for example, is that sex and wet dreams make a person vulnerable to disease, a belief not too different from one held in the West not all that long ago, that masturbation led to blindness!

Sexual abstinence, and thereby the retention of semen, was the way to power, as well as moral virtue. The man who holds in his sexual libido and the semen which embodies it will find that his body becomes suffused with radiant energy which will enable him to work all kinds of magic. The individual not only develops his psycho-sexual energy for his own spiritual benefit, but also, if he feels inclined, uses it as a power of good to others, as well as harm. Sexual intercourse was not the only way in which the generalized libido might escape. Sensuous pleasure of all kinds, such as food and clothing, should be abandoned as far as possible; the head shaved; the body tortured.

Gandhi seems to have had no such things in mind when he left India for England in 1888.

Gandhi showed considerable courage and determination in his decision to go to England. Ambition, adventurousness, it is never quite clear what his actual motives were, but he risked, and accepted, excommunication from his caste, though he did take the precaution of persuading his mother to give him permission to go across the 'black water'. This was only achieved through a vow made to his mother in the presence of a Jain monk, that he would not go near meat, liquor or women. Gandhi left behind in India his wife and two children.

The importance of Gandhi's stay in England lies not in the details of dress, his awkwardness, his search for vegetarian restaurants, even his calling to the Bar, but in the revelation he received there of his Hindu nature, and his commitment to it.

England gave him the opportunity to transcend the smallness of Hindu society, which defines a person not by his race but by his caste, sub-caste, and language group, and see himself as an *Indian*. This almost unique sense of racial identity was to give Gandhi power over millions of his fellow-countrymen, whatever their caste, sub-caste and language group, and make him the first leader in Indian history with universal appeal.

In London, Gandhi also became acquainted for the first time, and in an English translation, with the *Bhagavad Gita*, the most influential of all the sacred texts of Hinduism and the one most commented upon by Hindu sages and saints. The *Gita* forms a tiny part of the enormous epic (more than 200,000 lines) of the *Mahabharata*, an immensely complex and tedious account of the origins, course and aftermath of a great war, probably based upon a minor historical actuality enhanced by accretions of myth to the status of an epic. The *Gita* is a long philosophical dialogue between Arjun, the chief of one of the protagonists and his charioteer, the Lord Krishna. In it, the god's ostensible purpose is to persuade Arjun who, sickened by the thought of the carnage that must result from more warfare, has doubts about the wisdom of continuing the fighting, that he must fight on.

Essentially, the *Gita* is about duty, man's duty as laid down by his caste—Arjun is from the warrior caste, so his duty is to go to war. He must do his duty because God is unceasingly engaged in activity of one sort or another to keep the world in being. Man, therefore, by doing his caste duty and doing it well, comes to resemble God not only in his timeless essence, but in his activity. Simultaneously—and this is insisted upon almost *ad nauseam*—he must remain detached from the goal of his action. There is no salvation in good works, in what is being done, whatever the end. That is how God operates, and man must imitate him. Whatever he does, it is the *detachment* that counts, and in the desired and desirable state of total detachment, the works are irrelevant. The argument of Krishna is a formula for the dehumanization of man.

Gandhi interpreted the *Gita* into his own allegory of a duel between Good and Evil. His politics were an embodiment of that simplistic interpretation. Having defined British rule in India as evil, Gandhi fought it with the extremist vigour of one who was convinced he was on the side of the good. But he never forgot the necessity for detachment. Inner voices reminded him of it constantly.

Gandhi arrived in South Africa in 1893, still behind the mask of a lawyer, though a little uneasy in the role. When he returned to India for the last time in 1915, he was almost ready to assume the mask of freedom fighter, and the mantle of holy man; to move from barrister-at-law to Mahatma.

The details of Gandhi's life in South Africa are well known, the myth-makers defining the period as a sort of preparation in the desert for the real work to come. Glossed over is his failure to achieve anything of lasting value for the Indian community and his indifference to the plight of the indigenous African majority. Gandhi's sense of racial identity was reinforced in South Africa through personal humiliation. His ejection from a first-class railroad car by a European, the Mahatma later claimed, was a turning point in his life. It was also in South Africa that he took a final vow of celibacy, and invented the concept of *satyagraha*.

A great deal has been written about *satyagraha*, much of it by Western academics. About the time Gandhi conceived it, he described it.

Satyagraha is referred to in English as passive resistance. The term denotes the method of securing rights by personal suffering; it is the reverse of resistance by arms. When I refuse to do a thing that is repugnant to my conscience, I use soul-force. For instance, the Government of the day has passed a law which is applicable to me. I do not like it. If by using violence I force the Government to repeal the law, I am employing what may be termed body-force. If I do not obey the law and accept the penalty for its breach, I use soul-force.

As far as it goes, it is a very good definition, and the hundreds of thousands of words that have been expended upon 'explaining' *satyagraha* have not contributed anything of any value to it. Gandhi added religious jargon to the extant vocabulary of political action. Any strategy for weakness can offer only two choices, passive resistance or flight. *Satyagraha* supplied a supernatural justification for passive resistance. More importantly, *satyagraha* was a game between oppressor and oppressed. Its rules demanded that both sides play the game by them. *Satyagraha* was magic, Hindu magic, and if the other side did not recognize its nature, refused to follow the symbolic path, to exchange the necessary ritual, it could not work. It did *not* work in South Africa.

In 1909, Gandhi visited England in the hope of persuading the British government to help Indians in South Africa to acquire rights of citizenship. He failed to do so, and on the ship taking him back to South Africa, Gandhi composed a manifesto, *Hind Swaraj or Indian Home Rule*. This short pamphlet is a crucial document in any understanding of the nascent Mahatma. Its production at this time is proof that Gandhi had realized that his future, if any, lay in India and not in South Africa.

The manifesto is cast in the form of a dialogue between a 'reader' and an 'editor'. The 'reader' is obviously an amalgam of the sort of young Indian Gandhi had recently met in London who believed that Indian freedom could only be achieved by Western means, including terrorism of the sort associated by the British with the name of Tilak. The 'editor' is just as obviously Gandhi himself. The method of question and answer is used by Gandhi to attack and dispose of contemporary Indian leaders. Gokhale, the apostle of the gradual, is attacked, though obliquely:

We believe that those, who are discontented with the slowness of their parents and are angry because the parents would not run with their children, are considered disrespectful to their parents. Professor Gokhale occupies the place of a parent. What does it matter if he cannot run with us? . . . His devotion to the Motherland is so great that he would give his life for it, if necessary. Whatever he says is said not to flatter anyone but because he believes it to be true. We are bound, therefore, to entertain the highest regard for him.
Reader: Are we, then, to follow him in every respect?
Editor: I never said any such thing.

Tilak's clothes are stolen: 'We are day by day becoming weakened owing to the presence of the English. Our greatness is gone; our people look like terrified men. The English are in the country like a blight which we must remove by every means.'

But that means should not be un-Indian, to 'want English rule without the Englishman. You want the tiger's nature, but not the tiger; that is to say, you would make India English. And when it becomes English, it will be called not Hindustan but *Englistan*. This is not the Swaraj that I want.'

Anglophobia spews out. The British parliament produces nothing, because in a democracy there is no continuity, 'its movement is not steady, but is buffeted about like a prostitute'; the so-called 'free' Press is fundamentally corrupt; lawyers (!), doctors, trained in the West are using Western techniques to exploit India's people. The menace of Western civilization is all-pervasive, carried by the railway like some contagious disease to every corner of sacred India. Science and technology are not liberators but jailers.

The manifesto is a rodomontade against the modern world itself, presenting a vision of a lost Indian Golden Age:

> It was not that we did not know how to invent machinery, but our forefathers knew that, if we set our hearts after such things, we would become slaves and lose our moral fibre. They, therefore, after due deliberation decided that we should only do what we could with our hands and feet. They saw that our real happiness and health consisted in a proper use of our hands and feet. They further reasoned that large cities were a snare and a useless encumbrance and that people would not be happy in them, that there would be gangs of thieves and robbers, prostitution and vice flourishing in them and that poor men would be robbed by rich men.

The Luddite tone continues mercilessly: 'Machinery has begun to desolate Europe. Ruination is now knocking at the English gates. Machinery is the chief symbol of modern civilization; I am convinced that it represents a great sin.' And the answer? 'In our own civilization there will naturally be progress, retrogression, reforms and reactions; but one effort is required, and that is to drive out Western civilization. All else will follow.'

To drive it out needed selflessness and sexlessness:

> When a husband and wife gratify the passions, it is no less an animal indulgence on that account. Such an indulgence, except for perpetuating the race, is strictly prohibited. But a passive resister has to avoid even that very limited indulgence because he can have no desire for progeny . . .

After a great deal of experience it seems to me that those

who want to become passive resisters for the service of the country have to observe perfect chastity, adopt poverty, follow truth, and cultivate fearlessness.

Real Home Rule is possible only where passive resistance is the guiding force of the people.

The manifesto ends with a peculiar message for the British who, despite everything that has gone before, are not necessarily to be expelled from India. It is the first statement by the Mahatma that he needs the presence of the British in India in order to work out his plans.

Only on condition of our demands being fully satisfied may you remain in India; and if you remain under those conditions, we shall learn several things from you and you will learn many from us. So doing we shall benefit each other and the world. But that will happen only when the root of our relationship is sunk in a religious soil . . . If there be only one such Indian, he will speak as above to the English and the English will have to listen to him.

Gandhi forecast a form of collaboration and in a limited sense that is what he was to get.

FREEDOM FIGHTER

When Gandhi returned to India in 1915, he was received as a hero which 'emboldened me to think that I should not find it difficult to place my new-fangled notions before my countrymen'. He even accepted, with mocking deference, the advice of Gokhale, whom he had so savagely but obliquely attacked in *Indian Home Rule*, to avoid political activity and pronouncements until he had spent at least a year learning something about the India from which he had been long away. Gandhi travelled widely all over India by train, and in third-class compartments, the class of ordinary people. He was always to travel third class, though later it was to be a third-class special, a symbolic identification with the transit of the masses, but without the enforced discomfort.

In December of 1916, Gandhi attended a meeting of Congress. His own approach to political action seemed irrelevant to the two strains of nationalist thinking. The moderates, relying on rational argument to make their case, could not approve of mass protest as a means of persuading the British. Gandhi's support, however conditional, for the British Empire at war had no appeal for the extremists and the impatient young men. Gandhi made some impression at meetings of Congress, but did not inspire more than respect for his activities in South Africa. This apparent indifference did not worry Gandhi, for he sensed that his time would come. Observing the scene, he recognized the impotence of the essentially urban-oriented Congress.

The opportunity for Gandhi to arouse the rural masses came in 1917 when he was invited, and very reluctantly accepted, a

Government House, Calcutta, 1903

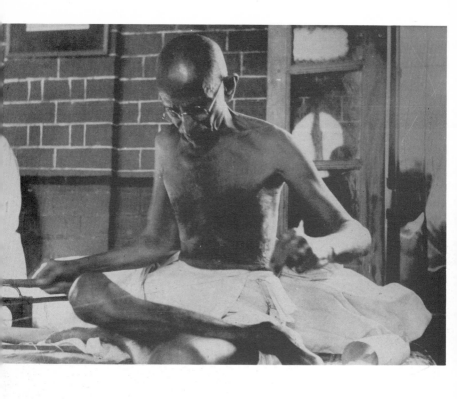

Gandhi at the spinning wheel at the Harijan Colony, Delhi

Gandhi on the eve of his historic Salt March, March 12th, 1930

Wavell inspects one of the state carriages used in peace time for state functions

Jawaharlal Nehru

Nehru and Jinnah walking in the gardens of Jinnah's residence, May, 1946

Jinnah, his daughter Fatima, and Lord and Lady Mountbatten at the formal ceremony marking the transfer of power from the British Raj to the dominion of Pakistan

Sardar Vallabhbhai Patel

request from one of the indigo workers of Champaran in Bihar, to champion their cause.

Champaran was remote, lying in the foothills of the Himalayas, close to the border with Nepal. The indigo crop, once one of great economic importance, had been almost completely devalued by the invention around the beginning of the century of synthetic blue dye. The local proprietors, mainly European, had concealed this fact from their tenants, and instead of demanding their rent in indigo, as had been the custom, began to require the whole in cash. Naturally, when the farmers learned that natural indigo no longer commanded a market, they were, quite rightly, convinced that they had been cheated.

The local authorities and the landlords soon acted against Gandhi. He was instructed to leave the district immediately. Gandhi refused to accept the order. 'Out of a sense of public responsibility,' he wrote to the magistrate who passed the order against him, 'I feel it to be my duty to say that I am unable to leave the district, but if it pleases the authorities, I shall submit to the order by suffering the penalty of disobedience. My desire is purely and simply for a genuine search for knowledge. And this I shall continue to satisfy as long as I am free.'

Gandhi appeared before the magistrate and submitted: 'As a law-abiding citizen, my first instinct would be . . . to obey the order served on me. I could not do so, without doing violence to my sense of duty to those for whom I came . . . I have disregarded the order served upon me, not for want of the respect for lawful authority, but in obedience to the higher law of our being—the voice of conscience.'

Gandhi prepared joyfully for arrest. But it was not to be; was not, perhaps, designed to be. Gandhi telegraphed his story to New Delhi. The viceroy intervened. Charges against Gandhi were withdrawn and an Agrarian Enquiry Committee was set up with the proto-Mahatma as a member. Though the farmers expected a refund of the rents they had paid, Gandhi was prepared to accept what they knew was less, but he considered more. Though the farmers received only a quarter of what they lost in cash, they received a total triumph of principle. There is no record of what the farmers really thought. In a subsistence economy, even a quarter's return is undoubtedly a profit.

Gandhi stayed in Champaran for some time. The farmers may have lost 75 per cent of their rent, but they were to be lectured and bullied into a new, more healthy, and certainly cleaner way of life. With the help of volunteers from as far away as Bombay, Gandhi tried to teach basic hygiene and sanitation, with simple medicine, mainly nature cures. Schools were established, soup kitchens offered and demonstrated how to make a simple and nutritious diet. Then Gandhi left. With the departure of the magician and his assistants, the ensorcelled were released from the spell, and the farmers and peasants of Champaran went back to their old ways. There is no reliable evidence that Gandhi thought constructively about them again, though he often quoted the Champaran affair as a victory for his new style of action.

While at Champaran, Gandhi had received a call for help in taking up the grievances of mill-workers in the industrial city of Ahmedabad in Gujarat. It was there that he first used the fast as an intimidatory weapon. While in Gujarat he also supported a no-tax campaign by peasants in the Kheda district. For Gandhi all these were experiments in arousing mass action. They were also significant in bringing two very different men into Gandhi's orbit. The Kheda affair brought Vallabhbhai Patel, the son of a poor farmer but by then a rich and successful lawyer in Ahmedabad. Patel was to become the organizer of the Congress campaign against the British, and after independence the most powerful force in Indian politics until his death in 1950. Champaran, which displayed Gandhi as a man of action, came to Jawaharlal Nehru as a revelation, and prepared the way for the commitment not only to the nationalist cause but also to Gandhi.

The times were certainly ripe both for revelation and commitment. The initial enthusiasm of Indians for the war, which in the light of later events now seems so improbable, had drained away as the fighting dragged on. The Home Rule League agitation had worried the government and there were growing signs that terrorism was about to emerge once again. The country was uneasy. An influenza epidemic originating in Europe spread to India and resulted in some twelve million deaths. The year 1918 saw the failure of the monsoon in some parts and floods in others, both producing a poor harvest. Food prices rose steeply. Indian soldiers, who had been hastily demobilized in case they should use their weapons against their officers, had taken their grievances back to the villages. In the cities, despite the enormous profits made by industrialists, both British and Indian, wages had been kept low while the conditions in which the worker had to live became progressively worse.

Even the certainty of political reform had contributed to apprehension. In October 1917 the then secretary of state for India, Edwin Montagu, a liberal of almost classic naïveté, had visited India and the consequence had been that the British government had decided upon a series of reforms unprecedented for a colonial power. Earlier constitutional changes had been based upon a limited representation for the expression of Indian opinion but none for legislative authority. The new reforms, though they were decried by Indian nationalists and socialists in Britain, were sensational in their implication. For the first time an imperial power had declared that some of its non-white colonial subjects were capable of operating self-government.

The reforms, when their contents were revealed, did not, of course, include *complete* self-government. But they did grant a division of powers. The central executive remained responsible only to the secretary of state in London, but legislation was, in theory anyway, to be the function of a new legislative assembly and a council of state with elected majorities but also an 'official' or nominated bloc. To balance this there was the proviso that if the legislature refused to pass an important bill the viceroy had the authority to bring it into effect by an executive act. The provinces were also to have legislative councils and the central government would give up some of its powers to these bodies. This devolution covered both finance and administration and to a certain extent the provinces would become self-governing. But again, that government was a division of power. The actual administration was apportioned between the elected council and the governor. Finance, justice and the police remained the governor's exclusive field while the elected ministers were to be given such things as education and public health. The electorate was to be increased from that granted by the 1909 reforms, though it was still subject to a sliding scale of property qualifications. The number who would be able to vote for the provincial councils would be about five million, for the central legislative council nearly one million and for the council of state a select group of some 17,000.

In spite of the encumbrance of so many checks and balances, the reforms were a real move forward. Many nationalists, including Gandhi, thought the changes reflected a new British attitude to India. Others, however, were not so sure. Among these the Muslims in Bengal, for example, were already angry and anxious over the reunification of Bengal. After the partition they had been given many concessions by the British in order to build up opposition to the almost entirely Hindu agitation against it. A larger proportion of posts in the provincial Civil Service had been allotted to Muslims and substantial funds had been made available for Muslim education. In 1909 they had received the grant of separate electorates in order to protect their community interests against the Hindu majority.

Then in 1911 the British had seemed to capitulate to Hindu extremism by reuniting Bengal. It was this as well as other factors, in particular the death in 1915 of the most influential old-style Muslim leader, which had led to the alliance between the Muslim League and Congress at Lucknow in the following year.

In order to achieve the Lucknow alliance, Congress had agreed to the principle of separate electorates for minorities in any future reforms. But Bengal had a Muslim majority, as did the Punjab. There the Hindu minority was to be protected by what was in fact overrepresentation for the minority. When agreed, this concession had seemed only academic but with the announcement of new reforms, the Muslims of Bengal realized that they would suffer. Bihar, which had presented Gandhi with his first exercise in agitation in India, had also a few months before been giving Muslims a foretaste of the future. In September 1917 the Hindus of the Shahabad district had attacked Muslims performing their traditional cow-sacrifice and the result had been communal violence on a scale previously unknown in British India. It seemed to many Muslims that this was a foretaste of Hindu Raj: the rule of the majority. Coupled with statements by the viceroy and the secretary of state that separate electorates were incompatible with parliamentary democracy, Muslims in Bengal became convinced that the new reforms were a threat not only to their communal identity but to their lives.

The reaction of some Muslim leaders was of great consequence to the future of the freedom struggle. In September 1918 a Muslim mob was incited to attack the houses of non-Muslim money-lenders and others, in a district of Calcutta. The ground had been prepared by stories of offensive references to Islam in Hindu newspapers. An attempt to stop a mob marching on Government House to present a petition dissolved in violence. In the end Calcutta was given over to three days of lawlessness, loot and arson. It was perhaps the first time in British India that a violent mob had been organized for specifically political purposes. The aim of the leaders was to direct violence against the non-Muslim community for the sole purpose of influencing the British. Their success in arousing mob violence revealed that there was mass discontent which could be manipulated by unscrupulous politicians for personal or communal advantage. The techniques for the communal disturbances of the coming years had been established.

Overwhelmed by a feeling of insecurity, the government of India decided to protect itself by taking special powers. The report of a commission of inquiry under Mr Justice Rowlatt into what the government called 'criminal conspiracies' was published shortly before the report of the secretary of state on the proposed reforms. The Rowlatt Report advocated sweeping security measures, including the trial of political cases without a jury and the weapon of preventive detention without any trial at all. The report was received with dismay by virtually every level of informed opinion in India—except, of course, the British. Of the nationalist leaders only Gandhi took positive action. He called upon the viceroy to refuse to authorize the security ordinances. When this appeal went unheeded he formed a Satyagraha Society whose members would take a pledge to disobey the law as an act of passive resistance.

The protests against the new security measures took place on two levels. Gandhi, in order to give drama and a nexus to acts of non-cooperation, proclaimed 6 April 1919 Satyagraha Day. There would be a *hartal*, or total suspension of business; protesters would fast and mass meetings would be held. On another level, and probably without Gandhi's knowledge, Congress workers were spreading alarmist propaganda. Rumours were set about that the government would be empowered by the new laws to 'inspect' a man and a woman before marriage. Another provision, it was said, restricted to two the number of plough-bullocks a peasant could own. Such rumours grew and multiplied, especially in the Punjab, the province from which a large majority of the rapidly demobilized soldiers had been recruited. Soon there were outbursts of popular indignation.

Most of the rioting, which was virtually confined to the Punjab and parts of western India, was spontaneous and characterized by racial and communal hatred. The government overreacted to Satyagraha Day and on 9 April Gandhi was arrested, though soon released. His detention provoked serious rioting in Bombay and Ahmedabad, and Gandhi, horrified by the violence that broke out, called off the campaign. But, as he was to learn again and again, violence once begun could not be called off. In the Punjab the administration, determined upon a show of force, arrested two popular Congress leaders on 10 April and when a crowd began a protest march on the European section of the city of Amritsar, the police opened fire. Turned back, the crowd looted two banks and burnt the railway station. Four Europeans were murdered by the mob and others beaten up, including a woman missionary who was left for dead. The military commander, Brigadier-General Dyer, managed to restore order and all public meetings and assemblies were banned.

Despite the ban, on 13 April a large crowd estimated at some 20,000 men, women and children gathered in an enclosed space known as the Jallianwala Bagh. When he heard of this, General Dyer went personally to the spot with ninety Gurkha and Baluchi soldiers and two armoured cars. As the entrance was too narrow for the armoured vehicles to pass through, he used them to block the only exit. He then ordered the crowd to disperse. It does seem likely that Dyer, who was a stranger to Amritsar, did not know that there were no other convenient exits from the Jallianwala Bagh, and that, when the crowd did not disperse because it could not, he panicked. Without warning, Dyer ordered his soldiers to shoot into the crowd. He admitted later that he fired all the ammunition he had with him and then withdrew, leaving, according to official estimates, 379 dead and 1,200 wounded. The armoured cars were left blocking the entrance so that no one could leave and no medical aid could get in. Dyer's action was given the approval of the governor.

The following day, a mob rioting and burning at another spot was bombed and machine-gunned from the air. On 15 April martial law was declared and not lifted until 9 June. During this period, Indians were forced to walk on their hands and knees past the spot where the woman missionary had been attacked and, according to the report of the Hunter Commission which inquired into the disturbances, public floggings were inflicted for such minor offences as 'the contravention of the curfew order, failure to salaam to a commissioned officer, disrespect to a European, taking a commandeered car without leave, or refusal to sell milk . . .'. The commission, which was set up in October 1919 with four British and four Indian members, only criticized Dyer's actions in the mildest terms as 'unfortunate' and 'injudicious'. Indians considered them a profound insult to their self-respect and pride.

It took some time for the news to reach the rest of India, as the Punjab government had imposed a strict censorship. But when it did, there was a thrill of anger and resentment. In some there was also a terrible disillusion. Gandhi's response was immediate and precise. There could be, he declared, no 'cooperation with this Satanic government'.

At the end of 1919, Congress held its annual session in Amritsar. In this emotive atmosphere the call was for positive action once again and the rejection of the forthcoming reforms. But Gandhi, who had been horrified by the violence that had emerged out of his campaign against the security laws, surprised and even shocked the delegates by calling for moderation, the acceptance of the reforms and participation in the working of them. Congress members had not yet learned the essential elements of the Gandhi style. Indeed, there was no reason why they should have done, for they had only once been displayed in the hurried calling off of the *satyagraha* campaign earlier in the year.

It was to be some time before the more astute Indian nationalists grasped the fact that the Mahatma had no policy, that he did not look to the future with logic and carefully formulated plans. His response was only to the present. For him, the future consisted only of a present that had not yet presented him with its problems. Gandhi was never aware of the reality of historical development. True to the Hindu spiritual tradition, he was consciously aware of *eternity*, but *time* was of no consequence. This was both his strength and his weakness. He was abnormally sensitive to the temporary and unpredictable mood of the Hindu masses. They learned to recognize this mysterious gift and gave him their allegiance. But his constant reaction to the shifting and disconnected elements that made up the present was to give to the Indian National Congress a spasmodic, unexpected and unforeseeable movement which disconcerted both the British and his own more intellectual followers.

In January 1920, true to his style, Gandhi again changed his mind. One of the reasons was the hero's welcome given to General Dyer on his arrival in England even though the government of India had disowned him and forced his resignation from the army. Another reason was the rejection by the British government of Indian Muslim protests over the terms of the peace treaty with Turkey, which had sided with Germany. Indian Muslims, growing more conscious of their minority status in their own country, had begun to look outside India to the wider Muslim world in the hope of gaining some sense of a larger identity. The highest religious office in the Muslim world was that of the Caliph of Islam, a title held by the Sultan of Turkey. The decision by the Allies to abolish the office of Caliph aroused considerable anger in India for it was taken as an insult to the faithful as well as being a violation of a pledge given by the British prime minister, Lloyd George.

The emotional effect of this was canalized into the formation of a political organization by two brothers, Muhammad and Sharkat Ali. The Khilafat movement, as it was called from the Indian word for caliphate, attracted widespread support, but more important still was its alliance with Congress. Gandhi recognized that the Khilafat issue could be used as a means of uniting Muslims and Hindus in common cause against a government which had shown so much disregard for the feelings of Indians of both religions. Gandhi was able to bring the two separate issues of the Amritsar affair and the campaign against the abolition of the Caliphate together and direct them towards the shared goal of *swaraj* or independence.

Gandhi convinced the Khilafat leaders more quickly than he did those of Congress. Most were with him on the matter of non-cooperation, but many were against both his bid for leadership and his technique of non-violence. To some, Gandhi appeared to be both obscurantist and reactionary. Just as many nationalists had taken their life-style from the West, so they had taken their political vocabulary, too. Gandhi was now using Indian words and Indian images to describe the aims of the freedom movement. He spoke always of *swaraj* and not of 'self-government'. He called not for the acceptance of the institutions of the British, even if their working was handed over to Indians, but for national reconstruction. He wanted new institutions created to take their place. He demanded not the boons of Western reforms but a reformation of Indian society. This, he claimed, could best be achieved by Congressmen leaving the cities and helping to set up cottage industries! The local manufacture of cotton goods should be revived and the spinning wheel become the symbol of India's new life. The wearing of homespun cloth would be a gesture of rejection as well as an affirmation of Indianness.

Gandhi's approach was frankly anti-intellectual. He demanded that imported European ideas be given up in the same way as imported European cloth. In 1920 he was proposing a complete reversal of the previous trends of Indian nationalism. He held up his own life and commitment as the *only* example to be followed: back to simplicity of living so that the individual could be free from the tyranny of material possessions, the renunciation of non-essentials so that there could be a total dedication to the struggle against foreign rule. Naturally, he was opposed inside Congress by those who disliked his views or believed them to be the wrong ones for India. But Gandhi was already attracting the allegiance of groups who had never participated in the nationalist struggle before and, more significantly, was doing so on an all-India scale. The majority of his opponents drew their support from specific regions and no others. Congress had hitherto been an alliance of regional leaders. Gandhi demanded something new—national leadership and a leadership without question. 'So long as you choose to keep me as your leader,' Gandhi told a meeting early in 1920, 'you must accept my conditions, you must accept dictatorship and the discipline of martial law.'

The beginning of the non-cooperation campaign was set for 1 August 1920; at the session of Congress held at the end of the year, Gandhi became the acknowledged leader and the movement began to take on the images and symbols he had started to make peculiarly his own. But one important member of Congress was driven away, never to return. Muhammad Ali Jinnah left for the political wilderness out of which he was to emerge as the enemy of the Mahatma and the architect of India's partition.

Gandhi's first exercise in 'civil disobedience' soon degenerated into violence and he called off the campaign. The violence, however, could not be called off, and after a particularly ferocious rebellion by Muslim peasants in South India, directed not against the government but against Hindus, the fragile thread of self-interest joining Hindus and Muslims snapped. Extremists from both sides now began to organize large-scale rioting, and, from 1922 onwards, bloody conflicts

between Hindus and Muslims became a regular feature of
Indian life. Gandhi antagonized Congress by publicly confessing the failure of the civil-disobedience movement and he was
only preserved from utter defeat by being arrested by the
British. He was sentenced to six years' imprisonment, but was
released on grounds of ill-health after serving only one.

Gandhi's contribution to the nationalist movement after his
release was almost entirely confined to praying and advocating
the virtues of hand-spinning. Though the latter was given a
certain propaganda value by the boycott of foreign cloth and the
wearing of homespun as a sort of nationalist uniform, it was
essentially an example of Gandhi's naïveté about economics.
Certainly it had little value in the struggle against the British
when Gandhi insisted that one of the qualifications for membership of Congress would be proof of spinning a fixed quota
of yarn. Many thought Gandhi's preoccupation with spinning
ludicrous. As the great Bengali poet, Rabindranath Tagore,
replied when Gandhi advised him to use the spinning wheel for
half an hour a day, 'Why not eight and a half hours if it will help
the country?'

The British felt that they had little to fear from Gandhi
himself, for they soon recognized him for what he was—an
anti-Western reformer. As long as Gandhi was in control of
Congress, they knew they had an ally. As long as civil disobedience remained non-violent, it did not greatly worry the government. Who was hurt by non-cooperation, anyway? Only the
Indians. Gandhi's whole aim was to minimize violence; the
government's was the same. The British were still capable of
suppressing a few outbreaks of small-scale violence, but if once
Gandhi ceased to dominate Congress, the machine he had
built up might well be used by more dynamic and violent
people. A full-scale rebellion could not be crushed. So the
government obliged Gandhi by treating him with considerable
respect—jailing him occasionally to keep up appearances
—while they took much more positive action against terrorists

and those Western-style revolutionaries whom they really feared.

Civil disobedience had been called off when it reached the edges of rebellion. Gandhi, who had sought to blackmail the British through an assault on their consciences, had been repulsed. He once told an English friend:

> An Englishman never respects you until you stand up to him. Then he begins to like you. He is afraid of nothing physical, but he is very mortally afraid of his own conscience if you ever appeal to it and show him to be in the wrong. He does not like to be rebuked for wrong doing at first; but he will think it over and it will get hold of him and hurt him till he does something to put it right.

In this, as in many of his other beliefs, Gandhi was wrong. In India, the moral content of British rule could not be reached by blackmail, for it had become petrified into a system. In Britain, there was merely indifference. In fact, the conscience of the British would have been much more quickly aroused if there had been widespread rebellion in India and a consequent attempt to suppress it. Gandhi and his methods were not understood. All that was recognized was that he was harmless.

In November 1927, the *Times of India* wrote of the 'completeness of the Congress collapse, the utter futility of the Congress creed, and a total absence among Congress supporters of a single responsible political idea'. And this seemed to be the truth.

A clause in the reforming Government of India Act of 1919 provided for a commission of inquiry after ten years to review the working of the Act. In November 1927 the commission arrived in India. The date had been brought forward primarily because it seemed possible that a Labour government might be in office in 1929, and at least one member of the Conservative cabinet actually believed that the Labour Party meant what it said about India's right to self-government. Far better, thought Lord Birkenhead, the secretary of state for India, to set up the commission early and give the impression that the Conservatives, too, were interested in India, so interested as to be prepared to bring forward the date by nearly two years. It was this same Birkenhead who had been the only member of the cabinet to oppose the reform of 1919, and he was determined that there would be no more if he could help it. So that the commission could be kept as much on his side as possible, it had to consist of members of the British parliament. The Labour Party co-operated by choosing only obscure back-benchers as their representatives. But one of these was a certain Clement Attlee, and his experiences were to have direct effect on the decisions he took nearly twenty years later as prime minister. The chairman of the commission was Sir John Simon, a lawyer delighting—if such a warm attitude can be attributed to such a cold temperament—in the passionless world of legal precedent. He as an ideal choice, for it was unlikely that even the vaguest suggestion of any sort of radical view would ever cross his mind.

The British in India were delighted at the all-British composition of the commission. Indians, on the other hand, held it to be racial discrimination. It seems probable that senior British officials hoped the exclusion of Indians would provoke criticism from the Hindu Congress, to which Muslims would react by supporting the commission, and that in turn, Congress fears of Muslim influence would prevent Congress from boycotting it. If this was indeed so, it merely confirms how little the administration understood the immense change that had taken place in Indian nationalism since 1919.

Gandhi remained quiet but Congress did not, for it viewed the commission as an insult that could be used to revive Congress purpose once again. The younger Nehru put forward a number of resolutions in the Madras session of Congress, and all of them were passed, including one which called, not for dominion status, but for independence. Nehru, however, suspected that his resolutions were accepted because they were not understood, and he was probably right. In the meanwhile, virtually all shades of Indian opinion had united against the commission. The Muslim League, however, was divided, and one group, headed by M. A. Jinnah, supported a Congress decision to boycott the commission. 'Jallianwalla Bagh was physical butchery', he said. 'The Simon Commission is butchery of our soul.'

The government of India, now seeking some way to appease Indian opinion, suggested that the commission should associate itself with a body of representatives from the Indian legislative assemblies. *The Times* in London thought this too generous, and even Attlee apparently thought it perfectly reasonable. The nationalists rejected it. But in the first two months of its visit, the commission was met by only a rather half-hearted boycott, and a less refrigerated personality than Simon might have broken it with a little display of human warmth. He had not, however, been chosen to be friendly to Indians. He even believed that the government of India was hostile to him, as it did not prevent such demonstrations as there were. However, this calm did not last, and demonstrations increased. A time bomb was set off in a train when the commission arrived in Bombay, and the police began to act against demonstrators. In one scuffle, a veteran nationalist, Lala Lajpat Rai, who was already fatally ill, received a blow and died soon afterwards.

The commission continued its 'blood-red progress', as Gandhi described it, throughout India, understanding little of what they saw. Congress published a report calling for immediate dominion status and outlining, in considerable detail, the sort of constitution the nationalists required. The report was submitted to an all-party conference in August 1928 and immediately resulted in a schism. Jawaharlal Nehru and his friends would not vote for it as it would commit them to the demand for dominion status. The report's attempt to solve the 'communal' problem only exacerbated it, and the Muslims now closed their ranks, demanding the continuance of separate electorates and a federal constitution in which Muslim-majority areas would have complete autonomy.

Gandhi had viewed the report as the instrument of an 'honourable compromise' with the British, yet the instrument had broken even before it could be used. Under pressure from Gandhi, the younger Nehru agreed to wait and see if the British would accept the report by the end of 1929. If they did not, then would be the time to organize civil disobedience. This was a tactical error, for it served a warning upon the government of India without having any effect on the government in London. The Muslim League also took it as a warning. Jinnah now became the dominant figure in the League and the road to the partition of India opened up. 'This', said Jinnah, 'is the parting of the ways', and he was right. Hindu–Muslim conflict was to continue to the very end, and its legacy still divides India and Pakistan today.

To those who rejected both the methods and the rationale of the Gandhian approach, there seemed no alternative but violence. Terrorism reappeared. In Lahore, a police officer, believed to be the one who had struck Lajpat Rai, was murdered. In April 1929 two bombs were thrown in the Legislative Assembly in Delhi. No one was hurt, but the two men responsible were hailed as heroes. A wave of terrorism broke out in Bengal, that epicentre of extremism, and the government took to itself wide-ranging powers of arrest and imprisonment. There were strikes, not always peaceful, in the Bengal jute mills and in Calcutta the scavengers stopped work. In Bombay, 100,000 workers walked out and brought the cotton industry of that great city to a standstill. The government responded by arresting the labour leaders and charging them with conspiracy and sedition. The trial, which was an attempt to crush a non-existent communist menace, went on for four and a half years and was conspicuous for its perversion of the law of British India, let alone of natural justice.

While the government's executive arm was suppressing in one way or another the most militant opposition, the viceroy attempted to neutralize the more moderate elements headed by Gandhi. The viceroy, Lord Irwin, was a deeply religious man who reacted emotionally to what he believed to be the essentially moral content of Gandhi's ideas. He was, he said, prepared to meet Gandhi—critics called it 'taking tea with treason'—and discussions did take place. Gandhi seemed to think that Irwin's piety overruled his political sense and his loyalties, which were those of any other member of the British ruling class. Irwin was not in fact a free agent. The ultimate power of decision rested with the British government in London. Nevertheless, Irwin's gesture—unprecedented in the history of British India—was taken by Gandhi to be not only an indication of his own stature but of British weakness.

Irwin, however, was by no means a fool. Whatever the more blinkered of the British community in India might say, any evolutionary approach to constitutional change in India depended upon Gandhi, the apostle of non-violence. In what seemed to be a revolutionary situation, it was only sensible tactics to encourage one who hated revolution and could carry the masses with him. It was necessary, Irwin thought, to strengthen Gandhi's hand. The viceroy's first step was to make a public statement of the sort that no viceroy had ever made before. He had, he said, a double duty to perform: to carry on the king-emperor's government and to serve as an intermediary between India and Britain. Privately, Irwin suggested to London that a declaration should be made immediately that dominion status for India was also the goal of the British government. This was too much for Lord Birkenhead, the secretary of state.

Changes, however, were in the air. The Conservative fears that a Labour success at the polls was imminent were proved correct. In the summer of 1929, the second Labour government in Britain's history took office. The prime minister was Ramsay Macdonald, who a few months before, on taking office had declared: 'I hope that within a period of months rather than years there will be a new Dominion added to the Commonwealth of Nations, a Dominion which will find self-respect as an equal within the Commonwealth. I refer to India.' Gandhi, responding to the call of the immediate present, had welcomed the statement. Others, including Jawaharlal Nehru, had been sceptical. In August 1928 he had referred to 'the sanctimonious and canting humbugs who lead the [British] Labour Party' and saw no reason now to change his mind. For a while it seemed that Nehru was wrong. In October 1929 Irwin made a rather vaguely worded statement which confirmed that the goal was indeed dominion status. Gandhi praised Irwin's sincerity and joined a conference of leaders from all parties called by the viceroy at the end of December. The morning it met, a bomb destroyed part of the viceregal train. The viceroy was unhurt.

The terrorists showed a greater awareness of reality. When Ghandi insisted that Congress had only agreed to join in the conference on the understanding that another conference would be called in London to frame a dominion constitution for India, Irwin told him that he was not empowered to make such a promise. The Congress delegates left Delhi, realizing at last that the British Labour Party was just like any other political party. Promises made in opposition had a habit of losing substance when office was achieved. The viceroy did, however, invite Congress leaders and others to attend a Round Table Conference in London in the following year.

Congress preferred to have nothing to do with the so-called Round Table Conference which the British Labour government had decided to summon in 1930. It now demanded independence without any qualification of dominion status and decided upon a campaign of civil disobedience, but these resolutions were passed in the face of considerable opposition which was overcome only by the still immense prestige of Gandhi. 'I have followed the Inner Voices', he proclaimed, and there were none authoritative enough to question whether he had heard the voices aright. The real questioning took the form of continued terrorist activity—which frightened Congress more than the government.

Gandhi had thought long about the nature of the act of civil disobedience. He had learned that, to rouse the masses, it was necessary to use some symbol they could easily recognize. There was no point in slogans about dominion status, because the masses had no idea of what that was. Gandhi hit upon the salt tax. The production of salt was a government monopoly and, in 1930, half the retail price of salt represented tax. Everybody used salt, everybody paid the tax. Why not incite the masses to break the monopoly by making their own salt?

The Mahatma decided that he would perform a magical act at the side of the Arabian Sea, at the little town of Dandi, and that he and a few chosen followers would leisurely walk the 200 miles between the site and his ashram at Ahmedabad. Gandhi sent a letter to the viceroy, opening 'Dear Friend . . .', informing him that if by 11 March he had not accepted eleven proposals, Gandhi himself would break the salt laws. Irwin refused to receive such an ultimatum. On 12 March, Gandhi marched off, expecting to be arrested on the way. But the government of India decided to try non-cooperation itself, and instructed the provincial governments not to arrest Gandhi. If the law *was* broken, only Gandhi's lieutenants were to be arrested and the Mahatma himself was to be denied martyrdom. Finally, Gandhi reached the sea, ceremonially made his uneatable salt—and broke the law. The act received great publicity abroad, especially in America, where it appeared to have overtones of the Boston Tea Party. The government of India, however, had not sent a single policeman to watch this symbolic act. On the same day, salt was made at about 5,000 meetings throughout India; Congress gave five million as the official number of those involved, but anything in India can draw a crowd, and it is certain that the majority of those who attended the ceremonies did so as casual onlookers.

The government went on quietly arresting some of the leaders—Patel on 7 March, Jawaharlal Nehru on 14 April —but Gandhi remained free, even though the government called his acts 'rebellion'. The administration did not even deny Congress permission to use the telegraph and the mails. There was no doubt that the government sought to protect Gandhi's control over the civil-disobedience movement by eliminating those it thought might give the movement a violent direction and by acting with moderation so as to keep the effect of the salt march within bounds.

In part, the government's policy was a success, for Gandhi's campaign had so far inhibited other action. Gandhi's hold on the masses seemed to drain the vigour from more intelligent and dynamic minds. Though all the essential motives for modern rebellion existed in India at this time—chronic unemployment among the educated classes and squalid living conditions for the industrial proletariat—1930 was a year almost entirely free from labour unrest; Gandhi canalized revolt into quiet channels, and when he shook his fist, it contained a moral maxim, not a gun. The authorities were instructed by the government not to use the military to disperse crowds: Jallianwala Baghs in every town might be an incitement to uncontrollable violence. The police had to handle things with as few strong-arm tactics as possible. Congress, of course, claimed 'police brutality', but most of it was exaggerated—justifiably so, for it was useful propaganda.

Concealed behind the façade of Gandhi's great campaign, there were men who felt that general rebellion was the only way of getting rid of the British, and these men were preparing to strike a blow. In Bengal, with its tradition of revolutionary violence, an armoury was attacked and eight men were killed trying to defend it. On the other side of India near the north-west frontier, the city of Peshawar exploded into violence after the arrest of Abdul Ghaffar Khan, a Congressman known as the 'Frontier Gandhi'. Troops had to be called in and heavy casualties inflicted. Even worse, two platoons of a native regiment of the Indian Army refused to go to Peshawar to shoot their unarmed brethren. The ugly spectre of mutiny, a spectre the British had never been free from since 1857, now seemed to rise again. On 24 April conditions were so bad in Peshawar that the British were no longer in control of the city and it was not until British troops and aircraft arrived twelve days later that the city was reoccupied.

The government of India at last decided that it had to arrest Gandhi, because the impression was growing, mainly amongst government servants, that the administration was being weak. In fact, there was not much purpose in keeping Gandhi out of jail any longer. The peasants who were his instruments were all busy in the fields reaping the spring harvest and were certainly not going to desert that for mere civil disobedience. Early in the morning of 5 May, Gandhi was unobtrusively arrested. There were a few demonstrations—serious ones in Delhi and Calcutta—and the remaining Congress leaders called on all Indians to intensify the campaign. The government, freed from the moderation necessary when backing up Gandhi, replied with sharp oppression—five years' rigorous imprisonment for failing to give information to the police, seven years and a heavy fine for carrying a Congress flag.

The government of India, however, soon found its attention diverted to what looked like a new frontier war, for the Muslim tribesmen of the north-west were on the march again and there was considerable rioting in towns in the North-West Frontier Province. The government, on the advice of a Muslim member of the viceroy's council, offered local self-government and secretly encouraged the spread of propaganda which smeared Congress as a Hindu body, so helping to intensify Muslim separatism. The government believed, though no adequate proof has ever been forthcoming, that Congress had incited the tribes and paid them large amounts of money. It seems highly unlikely that such was the case, but the government was beginning to see Congress, like the devil, under every stone and behind every disorder. The government even went further; it declared the All-India Congress Committee an unlawful association, and arrested Motilal Nehru, the Congress president.

The arrests did not halt violence, which continued all over the country, though, generally speaking, at such a level as to be fairly easily controlled and suppressed. The boycott on foreign goods, which assured Indian businessmen that nationalism was good for them and their businesses, flourished while the import of piece goods and cigarettes dropped to nearly a quarter of the previous year's figures. The government could do very little about this, though in Bombay it confiscated Congress buildings and property. Larger bodies of police were raised—the British could still rely on plenty of recruits despite Congress propaganda—collective fines were imposed upon villages, and young offenders whipped.

In June 1930, the publication of the Simon Report had been received in India with enthusiastic indifference. In fact, its reception in Britain was much the same; it is, after all, rather futile to be concerned over the future of a still-born child. The Labour government dissociated itself from the report by announcing that Sir John Simon would not attend the Round Table Conference, and the prime minister did not bother to consult even those Labour members of parliament who had been on the commission! The problem now before the governments of Britain and India was how to get Congress to attend the coming Round Table Conference.

In November 1930, the first Round Table Conference met in London. The Indian delegates, carefully chosen, represented every special interest from the princes onwards—except the only effective nationalist organ, Congress. Obviously, the conference could be of little value, and in fact it brought about nothing except a new stage in the relationship between the princes and British India. But one thing the conference made clear, that all the delegates wanted responsible government in India. Congress, it seemed, was not alone; even those elements whom the British thought to be 'on our side' echoed Congress demands.

Irwin made an appeal to Gandhi, inviting him to co-operate in placing 'the seal of friendship once again upon the relations of the two peoples, whom unhappy circumstances have latterly estranged'. The sensation that resulted from this was caused not by its almost classic understatement of the real state of relations, but by the fact that it was made at all. Official opinion was shocked; the viceroy's words seemed almost treasonable. But the appeal was really only another expession of governmental support for Gandhi in his role as neutralizer of rebellion. It was precisely keyed to his emotional understanding—hate put aside, earnestness displayed, a 'change of heart' for all to see. This was exactly what Gandhi had foretold would take place, that the conscience of the British would be awakened. The Labour prime minister, Ramsay Macdonald, followed Irwin's appeal by stating a new policy for provincial autonomy, a federal legislature, and safeguards for minorities during a transitional period only.

On 25 January 1931, Gandhi and the more important Congress leaders were released from jail. To many British this was an outrageous act, implying that sedition had become respectable. Congress, however, accepted the release as a gesture of genuine good will. Gandhi explained, 'I am hungering for peace, if it can be had with honour.' 'Honour' is a curious word, especially when used in conjunction with 'peace', but to Gandhi it meant 'respect', and that was what seemed to be offered. Also, Congress was wearying of civil disobedience. The government did not seem to have been weakened by ten months of agitation, authority still remained in its hands, and the disease of religious conflict among Indians had, instead of being stamped out, in fact become more acute. Perhaps Gandhi was right after all.

Given power by the weakness of Congress, Gandhi stated his terms to the viceroy. He complained against 'police excesses' and demanded an inquiry; the viceroy, however, replied by appealing to him to forget the past and think of the future. Gandhi was apparently not prepared to do so, but, when matters seemed to have reached a deadlock from which neither side could break out, the moderate nationalists persuaded Irwin to invite Gandhi to come and talk to him.

The meeting that took place was almost entirely concerned with the past, and on all major current issues the viceroy was unyielding. Gandhi, however, was not. 'I succumbed,' he said later, 'not to Lord Irwin but to the honesty in him'; in doing so, Gandhi ignored the instructions to be firm that had been given him by the Congress Working Committee. The Indian government nevertheless conceded the right of peaceful picketing under certain conditions, and ordered provincial governments to take the first step towards releasing political prisoners. Gandhi agreed to stop the boycott of British goods and to halt civil disobedience, which had almost come to a standstill anyway; when this had been done, the government was to abandon punitive ordinances, cease prosecutions, and make a number of other concessions.

On the surface, it seemed that the viceroy had won all the advantages, particularly since Congress had agreed to attend the Round Table Conference in London. But Congress also gained, in prestige. The pact appeared as one between equals and implied acceptance of the fact that Congress spoke for at least a large proportion of the Indian people. Most British opinion in India considered that the viceroy had been foolish to parley with an already defeated enemy who was only playing for time. They did not realize what a brilliant tactical advantage Irwin had achieved in the results of the parley. Neither did the government in London.

In India, opposition was growing against Gandhi, but it was not particularly powerful. Nehru opposed the settlement, but he soon gave in, and a number of really dynamic Congressmen, who might have made things very uncomfortable for Gandhi, were not free to do so. Many nationalists thought the amnesty for prisoners was too narrow in scope and that those convicted of murder should also be freed, or should at least have their death sentences commuted.

The government, in its desire to encourage Gandhi, withdrew its special ordinances *before* the civil-disobedience campaign had actually been called off, and there followed a period of considerable confusion. Ambiguous statements filled the air and each side interpreted them in its own particular way. The fact that the so-called Delhi Pact had been made in a cloud of emotion did not contribute to verbal precision. But one thing at least was clear. Gandhi had established a firm basis for Congress *co-operation* with the British and, despite the events that succeeded the agreement, the British government also was more firmly committed to co-operating with Gandhi. Irwin had achieved a stay of execution—for the British—while Gandhi had succeeded once and for all in diverting Congress from any truly revolutionary path.

Congress met, in a 'festival atmosphere', at Karachi, and it was decided that Gandhi should attend the next session of the Round Table Conference. Gandhi, who went off to London with, as he put it, only God as his guide, found the conference preoccupied with the problem of minorities, and, in particular, that of the largest—the Muslims. When Ramsay Macdonald addressed the delegates as 'My Hindu and Muslim friends', Gandhi interrupted with 'There are only Indians here.' Though the prime minister retaliated by changing his form of address to 'My Hindu friends ... and others', Gandhi had stated his position and he clung dogmatically to the thesis that Hindu and Muslim were one and that Congress, whom he represented at the conference, was the only body which could speak for all India. He would therefore offer no constructive suggestions for reconciling differences with those who spoke for other interests. His mystical attitude was not well received, especially as he appeared to have little or no awareness of the problems involved; he seemed to think that, by ignoring them, he proved they did not exist. The only precise statement he made was that if India received self-government she would not necessarily leave the British Commonwealth! Those at the conference who represented minority groups, especially the Muslims, demanded that separate electorates be retained. Gandhi, whose indifference to reality had by now antagonized everybody, was firmly against it. The British government, seeing no possibility of sensible discussion on this point, announced that it would itself make a decision on the problem of minorities. Gandhi's reply was to leave for India.

Congress now determined to revive the civil-disobedience campaign and, in reply, the government arrested Gandhi, and, over the next few months, some 80,000 others. Congress itself was declared illegal and so were many other organizations associated with it. The velvet glove was off again.

The viceroy had displayed to the world that the British were still in control. The British in India—and the government in London—were pleased. They believed that Gandhi was no longer needed to help run the country. Furthermore, the Congress party's sense of purpose had been considerably eroded by Gandhi's 'accommodation' with Irwin, and the new civil-disobedience campaign was a failure. Acts of terrorism and communal violence still took place, but the mass of the people had had enough of living at the centre of a whirlpool. By the middle of 1932, a sullen peace had descended upon India.

In September 1932, Gandhi announced that he was about to begin a fast to the death. The issue he chose for this dramatic gesture was the announcement by the British government that it would grant separate electorates to Untouchables. These are the lowest class in Hindu society, so low that a caste Hindu could be utterly defiled by having his shadow pass over one of them. Untouchables did unclean jobs: the tanning of leather, the clearing away of excrement. Untouchables were denied entry into temples, the use of the same wells as caste Hindus, and were generally discriminated against both socially and religiously by the rest of Hindu society.

Gandhi's decision to fast was not that of a freedom fighter but of a religious leader. The Untouchables, despite the disgusting way in which they were treated by caste Hindus, were for the Mahatma part of the seamless garment of Hinduism. The suggestion that they should be cut out of it, even politically, was immoral. To prevent such a thing happening, he was prepared to die.

For many of Gandhi's colleagues, it seemed hardly the right issue to die for, however important it might be in itself. Yet, no appeal for *political* common sense could have any effect on the Mahatma. The struggle for independence had been subsumed in the desire for religious reform. The question of separate electorates gave way to an assault upon the Hindu conscience. Untouchability was an offence to Gandhi's concept of a clean and refurbished Hinduism. It mattered nothing to him that the Untouchables, constantly discriminated against, had through their leader, Dr Ambedkar, jumped at the chance separate representation offered to them to break away from the dominance of caste Hindus.

On 20 September the fast began. The British were not

[219]

particularly worried about it, though they would not like to have Gandhi die in jail. They were prepared to feed him forcibly if necessary, or under certain conditions to release him on the principle that he was much less dangerous alive than dead. The following day a conference of Hindu leaders met and some were allowed to visit Gandhi in prison. Attempts were made to put pressure on Dr Ambedkar, who was quite unmoved by Gandhi's fast. On the fifth day of the fast, however, Ambedkar gave way and agreed to reject the British government's award. He did so in return for a promise that the Untouchables would be given seats from those reserved for Hindus. By this agreement the Untouchables got twice as many seats as they would have had under the award! But for Gandhi and for caste Hindus, it meant that Hinduism was preserved.

For a while, too, it seemed that Gandhi's hope of reform in the way Untouchables were treated would be fulfilled. Temples previously closed to them opened their doors. The wells and the pasture lands from which they had been excluded were now offered to them with all the appearance of general repentance. But it was not to last. The emotion drained away in the fear that thirty million Untouchables might threaten the vested interests of caste Hindus. The temple doors closed again, tradition reasserted itself. The fast had indeed been a waste of time. It had also done real harm to the nationalist movement, for it was a diversion from the narrow road that led to freedom. The British recognized that Gandhi had once again co-operated in taking the fire out of their opponents.

But the Mahatma remained unpredictable. On 8 May 1933, still in jail, he announced yet another fast! The Inner Voices had spoken to him once again and this time they had even been precise about the period for which he must fast. It was to be twenty-one days, and the purpose—'self-purification'. This time the government had had enough. On the same evening, a communiqué was published stating that in view of the nature and object of the fast, it had been decided to set the Mahatma at liberty.

No one was more shocked than Gandhi. Prison was an almost essential backdrop for his personal drama. Now with his mind adjusted to fasting, he was to be virtually put out in the street. Reluctantly he allowed himself to be taken to a mansion outside Poona and there, despite the protests of followers and Congress leaders, went on with the fast. In return for his release he officially called off the civil-disobedience campaign, which had already died of exhaustion. For some reason, he still thought he had something to bargain with and announced that he was only *suspending* the campaign for six weeks and would reactivate it unless the government released the remaining political prisoners. But not even Gandhi could raise the Lazarus of civil disobedience and the government knew it.

The drama now became a farce. Gandhi ended his fast after the divinely ordered number of days. In June he extended the 'suspension' of civil disobedience for another six weeks and in July formally ended *mass* civil disobedience. The government was indifferent. Gandhi asked for a meeting with the viceroy. It was refused. At the beginning of August, now fully recovered, he offered individual *satyagraha*, was arrested, and then re-leased after three days with an order confining him to Poona. This he refused to accept and was arrested again and this time sentenced to one year's imprisonment. Back in his old cell he thought he could continue with his campaign against Un-touchability. Previously he had been treated with considerable tenderness; this time he was told that he would not be allowed to dictate the terms of his imprisonment. His reply was to begin yet another fast.

The trivialization of the technique was now complete, and even Gandhi was aware of it. The fast became an acceptance of failure. Within five days he was seriously ill and making no attempt to resist the effects of starvation. Again, the government decided to release him, to die, if he must, elsewhere rather than in a British jail. Gandhi was caught off balance. Again he was taken to the mansion outside Poona where his friends tried to convince him that he must really fight to live. The fast was over, but the effects remained not only on Ghandi's shattered body but on his mind. He was in despair and wanted to leave Congress and politics. Many Congressmen thought this would be the best thing for the nationalist movement.

There was no doubt that the majority of the Westernized intellectuals in Congress resented Gandhi's reactionary views, but there was very little they could do about him even if they wanted to. They very fact that they were intellectuals, with European-style opinions, was against them. The majority of Congress members did not even understand what these men were talking about, and those who did were usually businessmen who automatically reacted against the very mention of the word 'socialism'. The left wing too was convinced that the support of the masses was the key to political change. That support they could not hope to win by themselves. The equation was inescapable—Congress needed mass support to justify its claim that it spoke for India. Gandhi had mass support, therefore Gandhi must equal Congress.

In 1937 the government of India put into effect new reforms. By them, Indians were to be granted a large measure of self-rule, though at first confined to the provincial governments. Congress was divided on whether it should co-operate, but in the end the decision was made to give the system a try. Gandhi took no active part in the discussions that preceded the decision. He had resigned from Congress and spent most of his time on village-welfare schemes. But his spirit remained behind to influence people.

Congress was not a political party in any Western sense, nor, when it accepted office, did it operate in Western democratic terms. It had declared its aim as not to work the constitution, but to destroy it and thus bring independence nearer. But Congress had been elected on a platform which contained the promise of specific social and economic reforms and, when its ministers took office, they found themselves under pressure from their constituents to get on with the job of translating promises into reality. This brought a dilemma. To institute radical changes could only lead to the alienation of some special-interest group essential to Congress unity. Agricultural reform would have meant antagonizing landlords, industrial legislation would have threatened Indian big business. On the other hand, failure to initiate reform would imperil the masses' support of Congress. Furthermore, it would be a denial of Congress's avowed reasons for claiming that Indians could rule themselves better than the British. The strains inside Congress soon became severe and there is no knowing what might have happaned if the outbreak of World War II had not given Congress ministries an excellent excuse to resign. Otherwise, mass disillusionment would inevitably have grown, and Congress itself might well have split. Meanwhile, for a limited period, Congress leaders were in a position to control their members. They used coercion where possible and expulsion when necessary.

Many Congressmen resented being bullied from above and tried to force the Congress leadership into following a programme of radical reform. One in particular, Subhas Bose, saw behind this authoritarian rule the deadening hand of Gandhi, the Congress dictator.

Bose had his own view of India's future and that of the freedom movement. His activism had been rewarded with persecution by the British, and he had been forced to spend some years outside India. Returning in April 1936, having warned the British that he was coming, he was arrested immediately on arrival at Bombay. Bose's reputation abroad now rivalled that of Gandhi. Indeed, on the surface anyway, he was much the most attractive of Indian leaders. Through his writings and speeches Bose had also become a national figure.

At this stage Gandhi decided to give Bose the highest office in the movement and allow it to mellow his revolutionary zeal. Although Bose was very conscious of the need for Congress unity, he was not prepared to compromise his principles for it. He accepted the nomination for Congress president as a tribute to the ideas he represented so forcefully, and was determined to use his period of office to free Congress from the 'dead hand' of Gandhi. Gandhi was fully aware of this. Bose offered a real threat, not only to the unity of Congress, but to the Mahatma's dominant position.

Bose acted at first with great circumspection. His presidential speech contained no criticism of the Mahatma, no call for Congress reform. But he looked forward to the time when Congress would have achieved independence, and for this Congress must plan now. Once at the centre of things, Bose discovered that though he reigned as president, he did not rule. The old guard were firmly in control and apparently immovable. In his disillusion he felt isolated and useless. Gandhi had succeeded in emasculating this tiger from Bengal. Towards the end of 1938, however, Bose became convinced that war in Europe was not far off. He had always considered that, should Britain go to war, it was the duty of Indian nationalists to take advantage of its preoccupation elsewhere. Bose decided that he needed a second term as president of Congress.

Gandhi was not prepared to consider such a thing. He had avoided a direct challenge to his authority and it was now time for Bose to be put aside. The right-wing leaders headed by Patel now put up another candidate and issued a statement condemning Bose's determination to stand for election, as a threat to Congress unity. Bose refused to withdraw. Gandhi, who had taken no direct part in the controversy although he had been very active behind the scenes, openly came out against Bose in an article in his newspaper *Harijan* on 28 January 1939. 'Out of the present condition of Congress,' he wrote, 'I see nothing but anarchy and red ruin in front of the country.'

To the surprise of the right wing, Bose won the election by a majority of just over 200 votes. Gandhi took the result as a personal defeat. Bose was conciliatory, Gandhi firm in his opposition. Soon there came a pretext for all but three of the members of the Working Committee to resign. Bose was now in extreme danger. If Congress had to choose between him and Gandhi, it was obvious who would be the loser. He tried to approach Gandhi but—though the two men met for discussions at which Bose, realizing rather belatedly that there would be no national movement with any real popular support without the Mahatma, was conciliatory—Gandhi had no intention of co-operating with him. There was now no alternative for the rebel president but to submit his resignation.

Many Congressmen were soon condemning Bose as a fascist, but Bose replied that if fascists meant Hitlers, super-Hitlers, or budding Hitlers, 'then one may say that these specimens of humanity are to be found in the Rightist camp.' He now attempted to found a new left-wing organization, the Forward Bloc. This failed. It was, however, by no means the last that India was to hear of Subhas Bose.

Gandhi, whom so many both in India and abroad believed to be compounded only of sweetness and light, had, by the use of his overwhelming prestige and the sort of intrigue one would expect from Tammany Hall, succeeded in disposing of the only real opposition to his leadership.

13

GIANT KILLER?

The war that broke out in Europe in September 1939 caught the majority of Congress members unaware. Some, like Nehru, had seen the war coming, and had agonized over what should be done. Other Congress leaders did not share his torment—or his view of the world. They knew little of international affairs and cared even less. Their blinkered vision saw only the road to Indian freedom and to be over much concerned about a civil war in remote Europe seemed only a dangerous diversion. Their innocence was profound—and aggressive. What had Nehru's fears to do with them? There were others who welcomed the war, for it could be used to India's advantage. Subhas Bose saw Britain's troubles in Europe as an opportunity for India to snatch independence from the failing grasp of the conqueror.

The need for Congress to define its attitude was demanded on 3 September 1939 when the viceroy, as was undoubtedly his constitutional right, declared India at war with Germany and promulgated a number of ordinances giving himself special wartime powers. His action underlined the fact that however far India had been taken towards responsible government by the 1935 Act, it was the British who still ruled, and that in matters of life and death Indians were not even to be consulted.

The Congress Working Committee met on 8 September. There was no unanimity of opinion about what should be done. Bose, who has been invited to the meeting, called for instant and widespread civil disobedience. But he was alone in his belligerence. Most members wanted the Congress provincial governments to remain in office, and this could only be achieved by some sort of compromise with the British. Nehru, who was looking for any reasonable formula that would allow Congress to support the war, found himself on the side of the right-wing leaders. But even they were not thinking of total support. Gandhi was only for India's moral, not active and therefore violent, involvement in the war. Nehru maintained that fascism could not be fought with fine phrases.

But first the British had to be sounded out. Nehru drafted a 'war aims resolution' which demanded that the British should state what they were fighting for. If it was for things as they were, for colonial possessions and privilege, then Congress would not have anything to do with the conflict. On the other hand, should it be for democracy and *democracy for all*, then Congress would co-operate. Congress was not alone in wanting guarantees from the British. The Muslim League courteously informed the government that though it condemned Nazi aggression, it would require an assurance that no decision would be made about India without its approval. 'The Muslim League', it stated categorically, was 'the only organization that can speak for Muslim India.'

The government's reply to what was in effect a Congress demand for immediate freedom was bland and unaccommodating. All it was willing to promise was that *at the end of the war* it would 'be prepared to regard the scheme of the Act [of 1935] as open to modification in the light of Indian views'. But the British would make a gesture of good will: they would establish some sort of consultative body which would include the viceroy and representatives of various Indian political groups. This was too feeble to appeal to any of the Congress leaders, even Gandhi. A promise to discuss dominion status after the war and a consultative body shared with others was quite unacceptable. The Working Committee ordered the Congress provincial governments to resign. With some reluctance, the call was obeyed, and by 15 November all had given up office. The other non-Congress ministries remained where they were.

Despite the Congress action, attempts at compromise continued but there was no desire for a solution on the part of the
British. The viceroy, Lord Linlithgow, had an almost Victorian
attitude to Empire, and had no wish to see Indians rule
themselves. There also seemed no pressing reason for making
concessions. The war in Europe had come to a standstill after
the attack upon Poland. Britain remained strong and there was
certainly no overt threat in Asia. Nevertheless, the Viceroy was
not idle. He had a profound dislike of Congress, which he
considered a 'movement of Hindu hooliganism'. When Linlithgow heard of a meeting between Nehru and Jinnah that
gave the impression that a compromise was possible between
Congress and the League, he set out to cultivate Jinnah. One
result was that the League called for a 'day of deliverance and
thanksgiving' on 22 December to celebrate the resignation of
the Congress governments.

Congress met in session in March 1940 in an atmosphere of
frustration tempered by a desire for action. Once again it was
Gandhi's Congress. Though not officially a member, he was
the acknowledged leader behind whom everyone rallied when
it came to the point of no return. Though Gandhi stated
'Compromise is in my very being', he called for civil disobedience. But there would have to be a delay as the organization
was not yet ready for a non-violent campaign. Congress
agreed. Gandhi had their complete approval. It was almost like
old times. Any criticism inside Congress was unvoiced. Even
Nehru was silent and took no part in the proceedings. Subhas
Bose, who had called an 'Anti-Compromise Conference'
simultaneously with the Congress session, also demanded
action but immediately and with 'no rest or break, nor any
sidetracking as happened in 1932'. But the initiative was once
again with Gandhi.

The Mahatma did nothing. The inner voices were
apparently silent. But while Gandhi waited, the war in Europe
burst into shattering life. In April, Denmark and Norway were

invaded, then Holland and Belgium. As the Germans swept into France, the British forces were pushed to the sea, escaping in an armada of small boats from the beaches of Dunkirk in the early days of June 1940. It seemed to many that the Germans must be irresistible and that Britain would soon be invaded. What then would happen to India? Would the Germans take over? What was to be done? The British government in London had been aware of the dangers from the start of the German offensive, and the viceroy was instructed to do everything he could to unite Indians behind the war effort. That obviously included Congress. Linlithgow, however, was not prepared to make a move. In May his immobility was encouraged by the appointment as British Prime Minister of Winston Churchill, that arch-enemy of freedom for India.

The events in Europe came as a shock to the Congress leadership. Divisions immediately appeared. Nehru was strongly opposed to taking advantage of Britain in its hour of peril. Civil disobedience now would be like becoming allies of the Nazis. Gandhi too did not wish to embarrass the British when they were fighting for their lives. He was also well aware that if the Germans took over India there would be no possibility of a non-violent struggle for India's freedom. The revolutionaries would dominate the nationalist movement and there would be no place for him. Maulana Azad, then Congress president, disagreed with both Gandhi and Nehru. The British, by refusing the modest requests of Congress, had brought non-cooperation upon themselves. Why should Congress, having denounced the war as imperialist, now change its mind?

The Working Committee met in emergency session. There was a majority for negotiation with the British. The offer was once again of co-operation, but this time of *complete* co-operation. There were only two conditions: the declaration of Indian independence to take effect after the war and an all-party national government now as a token of that promise.

The armed forces would remain under the British commander-in-chief and the viceroy's position would be unchanged,
though he would be expected not to use his veto except in cases
of extreme emergency. The offer was made in all sincerity, a
feeling backed by genuine fear. For years Congress had
concentrated on its struggle with the British. It was a movement of parochial aims and parochial minds. Only a few
recognized that India was not isolated from the world outside
and that what went on there affected India too. The offer of
co-operation was made not to help Britain fight Germany but
to help defend India from attack.

The Congress offer also revealed a split with Gandhi. As
early as 1938 he tried to get Congress to agree with the
proposition that when India became free it would not have
armed forces. There had been some disagreement, but the
matter had been put aside without decision. Now it was necessary to define the Congress attitude precisely. Under the
influence of Nehru, Rajagopalachari and Azad, the Working
Committee, though accepting non-violent methods as suitable
for the struggle *inside* India, rejected them as a means of
national defence. This resolution was accepted at a meeting of
the All-India Congress Committee in July. Four members
of the Working Committee abstained from voting, and Abdul
Ghaffar Kahn, the 'Frontier Gandhi', resigned as a protest
against the jettisoning of 'non-violence'. Though Nehru tried
to soften the blow to Gandhi there was no doubt that Congress
had, for the first time since 1920, decisively rejected the
Mahatma.

The effect of the resolution upon the left wing of Congress
was immediate. Many of its leaders had already been arrested
and they looked to Nehru to defend the radical position. One of
the leaders of the Congress Socialist Party wrote to Nehru,
appealing to him to head the opposition against the offer of
co-operation with the British. Once again they had mistaken
their man. It is possible to see in this episode the hardening of

disillusion with Nehru which was to lead finally to the socialists leaving Congress immediately after independence. Many socialists had already come to distrust Nehru, and now it seemed that he had finally deserted them for co-operation, however limited, with the British. His reasons did not convince them.

There were, however, other parties with an interest in the sort of compromise that might be reached. Even Congress had recognized that a united front would make some difference. The Congress president, a Muslim, had approached Jinnah but had been rejected with the brutal words: 'Cannot you realize that [as Congress president] you are made a Muslim show-boy, to give it colour that it is national . . . ? The Congress is a *Hindu* body.' Jinnah particularly resented Azad being Congress president because he believed that all Muslims should be members of the League. In March, Jinnah had gone further and made what was later to be known as the 'Pakistan resolution'. 'Muslims', he had said, 'are a nation according to any definition of a nation, and they must have their homelands, their territory and their State.' This pretension had been dismissed as 'meaningless and absurd'. Why then should Jinnah co-operate with Congress?

The British took some time to answer the Congress offer. The viceroy consulted Jinnah and was told that there were conditions that had to be satisfied before the Muslim League would agree to join a 'national' government. First, the British must undertake to adopt no constitution, temporary or final, 'without the previous approval of Muslim India'. Secondly, in any wartime administration 'Muslim India must have an equal share in the authority and control of the Governments, central and provincial.' The positions of Congress and the League were obviously incompatible. The British response to Congress came in August. On the matter of independence, they would promise no more than that a representative body would be set up after the war to decide on a new constitution. In the meantime, they were prepared to invite a number of 'representative' Indians to join the viceroy's executive council and set up a War Advisory Board, with Indian members.

The British offer differed only in detail from that made in October 1939. But there was one clause which seemed to give to the Muslim League the veto for which it had asked. The British would not contemplate any transfer of responsibility to a system of government 'whose authority is directly denied by large and powerful elements in India's national life. *Nor could they be parties to the coercion of such elements into submission to such a Government.*' The offer was unimaginative—and unyielding. When the Congress leadership met on 15 September, the delegates were in a somewhat chastened mood. The panic which had marked the earlier meeting now seemed exaggerated. Germany had not invaded Britain nor had the British given in under heavy aerial attacks. The inflexibility of the government's August offer perhaps reflected the optimism of the British. There now seemed no alternative for Congress but to turn back to Gandhi. Nehru and the other members of the Working Committee moved into the background and the Mahatma took the stage again.

Gandhi, as usual, had no plans. In fact, he was extremely reluctant to take any serious action. For this there were two important reasons. He still hoped for a compromise with the British and he was not convinced that a civil-disobedience campaign would be effective. There was no issue on which to arouse the masses. Congress leaders might be concerned with independence, some of them even with anti-fascism, but these were matters which did not interest ordinary people. Though there had been some shortages of consumer goods after the outbreak of the European war and a rise in the cost of living, this primarily affected the minority middle class. The Indian peasant, constantly at war himself with poverty and starvation, felt very little difference in the texture of the battle for life.

In his endeavour to escape from the trap of ineffectiveness, Gandhi approached the viceroy at the end of September with a demand for freedom of speech to criticize the war, such criticism now being prohibited by ordinance. If this demand was granted, Gandhi wrote, there would be no need for civil disobedience. The viceroy refused—India was at war and there must be some limitation on opposition to it. The Mahatma now had no alternative but to start civil disobedience. He then chose the most ineffective method. There would be no mass *satyagraha*; only individuals would defy the law. Nehru found Gandhi's intention feeble, a sign of weakness. He was convinced that Gandhi the strategist was wrong but allowed himself to be won over by his devotion to the man.

The first protestor was to be Vinoba Bhave, a disciple of Gandhi who had tried to make himself into a simulacrum of the master. He made a simple statement which Gandhi had written: 'It is wrong to help the British war effort with men or money. The only worthy effort is to resist all war with non-violent resistance.' On the third occasion of making the statement in public, Bhave was arrested and sentenced to three months' imprisonment. The event caused no stir at all. No mention of it was made in the censored newspapers. For most Indians it was a non-event.

Individual *satyagraha* continued and so did the arrests, though sentences were mild. Then, in an endeavour to add a little drama, Gandhi informed the viceroy that members of the Congress Working Committee, the AICC, and members of the legislatures, would act in groups. By the end of January 1941 nearly 3,000 protesters were in jail. There was little excitement over the arrests, though the government now extended censorship to the mails. Apart from a truce over Christmas 1940, so the British could celebrate *their* religious festival, said Gandhi, the campaign went on, the clang of the prison gates silenced by censorship. It all seemed rather pointless and there was rising criticism inside Congress and a

[233]

growing desire to call off the campaign. Gandhi would have none of it. His 'moral protest', he insisted, was 'a token of the yearning of a political association to achieve the freedom of 350 million people'.

By the early summer of 1941, the campaign had all but died of its own accord. Political India seemed in the doldrums. Yet things were happening. The minority parties were still active. The Muslim League ministries still in power were not being particularly co-operative, mainly out of the conviction that the government would take no action against them. Moderate Indians were still trying to bring about a reconciliation between the conflicting parties, but they held the confidence of no one, not even the British. The government in London continued to reiterate its promise of full dominion status after the war—and implied that it could only be granted to a united India. The then secretary of state for India, L. S. Amery, reminded Indian nationalists that their duty was to 'India first!' This gratuitous advice provoked Gandhi into calling on the British to leave India and let Congress and the Muslim League work out their own problems. 'It may be,' he went on, 'that before we come to that happy state of affairs, *we may have to fight among ourselves.* But if we agree not to invite the assistance of any outside Power, the trouble will perhaps last a fortnight.' By 'fight' Gandhi probably only meant 'argue' but either way it seemed a very naïve proposition. Naturally there was no response from London.

In India there were increasing signs that the Muslim League was being advised on its policies by senior members of the British administration. The terms of the August offer, which had not been withdrawn, were very slowly implemented and it was not until July 1941 that Indians were appointed to the viceroy's executive council. When the names were made known, they turned out to be those of men of quality and experience but totally unrepresentative of the mainstream of Indian nationalism. From the nationalist point of view these men, however admirable in themselves, could be no more than puppets.

A few weeks later, any confidence in the honesty of British intentions that still remained received a further blow. The British and American governments represented by Winston Churchill and President Roosevelt issued a statement on their concept of the post-war world. This 'Atlantic Charter' became part of the war aims of the Allies. When the text of the charter was released, Indians welcomed the clause which claimed that both the signatories respected 'the right of *all peoples* to choose the Government under which they live; and they wish to see sovereign rights and self-government restored to those who have been forcibly deprived of them.' Indians were soon disillusioned, for Churchill hastened to make it clear that this clause only referred to European nations and that India was 'quite a separate problem'.

This qualification reminded some Indians of how the doctrine of self-determination enunciated by President Wilson in World War I had not applied to colonial peoples either. It seemed as if nothing had changed in the intervening years. An attempt by Amery to equate Britain's offer of an elected constituent assembly after the war with the terms of the charter was unconvincing. Even those Indians who had never ceased to believe in the sincerity of British promises began to have their doubts.

The pointlessness of Gandhi's *satyagraha* campaign led to bitterness and confusion in the Congress ranks. What was perhaps more important was that Congress had lost touch with the people. Recruits were flowing in to the British Indian army. Indian factories were working day and night producing war supplies for the Middle East and African fronts. Indian workers were receiving the highest wages they had ever had. Neither labourer nor factory owner, however nationalist he had once been, was prepared to give up this sort of prosperity. One Indian leader, recognizing that Indian freedom could no longer be fought for with any hope of success *inside* India, set off on a search for allies outside. Subhas Bose, gaining release from jail by threatening a fast to the death, escaped from house arrest in January 1941 and, after failing to interest the Russians in his plans, finally arrived in Berlin in March. But even his voice on the radio calling upon Indians to rise and help those who were willing to help them was heard by only a few, and where was the help he talked of anyway? It was nearer than anyone thought.

On 4 December 1941 the government unexpectedly released all the Congress prisoners, including Nehru. Three days later the Japanese attacked the American naval base at Pearl Harbor. The same day, Japanese aircraft bombed the American island of Guam, military installations in the Philippines and the British naval base at Singapore.

The speed and vigour of the Japanese offensive created a sense of urgency. In Congress the old panic revived, this time with greater intensity. The doctrine of non-violence was again thrown aside. Nehru openly stated his view that bombs could not be resisted by non-violent methods. The demand for some sort of co-operation with the British in the defence of India grew in strength, and Gandhi asked to be relieved of the leadership of Congress. This was accepted on 16 January 1942 when the AICC made another offer of conditional support to the British. Not all the members of the Working Committee were in agreement.

Rumours were going around that the split beween Nehru and Gandhi on policy had hardened into a parting of ways. Nehru denied it and, more significantly, so did Gandhi. The Mahatma went further and publicly stated what most Congressmen had come to expect: 'Jawaharlal will be my successor.' The relationship between them, he said, was a 'union of hearts'. He knew, Gandhi went on, 'that when I am gone he will speak my language'—a highly improbable prophecy which was, perhaps, more a statement of hope. This confirmation of

Nehru's position was not welcome to everyone but the opposition was concealed while Gandhi was alive. At the time, it did not matter much, for should the Japanese invade India, Nehru and Gandhi would probably both be replaced.

In the middle of February 1942 the 'impregnable' fortress of Singapore fell, and in Burma the British were soon on the retreat. What was happening was almost inconceivable. The British Empire, so unyielding to Indian nationalism, was crumbling before the attacks of the Japanese. It seemed to many that Subhas Bose had been right: non-violence had only hindered the march to freedom. Yet in many ways the imminence of deliverance by the Japanese was not taken seriously. The Muslim League was more concerned with fighting Congress. The extreme communalist organization, the Hindu Mahasabha, defied the Muslims to come out and fight in the streets. As the Japanese marched on, the politicians screeched at one another.

On 8 March, the tide of Japanese conquest flowed over Rangoon, the capital of Burma. Four days later Winston Churchill announced in the House of Commons that a socialist member of the war cabinet, Sir Stafford Cripps, would go to India to 'satisfy himself upon the spot by personal consultation that the conclusions on which we are all agreed and which we believe represent a just and final solution, will achieve their purpose'. It was, said Churchill, the desire of the British government to 'rally all the forces of Indian life to guard their land from the menace of the invader'. There were many, including Churchill and the government of India, who would have preferred to keep the nationalist leaders locked up for the duration of the war but there were some doubts in Whitehall as to whether the authorities in India, with the Japanese at the gates, would be able to suppress an internal rebellion if such a thing followed the arrests. Undoubtedly there were extremists willing and anxious to act as a fifth column for the Japanese. Churchill saw the attempt at reconciliation as leading to a possible truce, which would leave the British to get on with the task of defending India.

There were also domestic reasons for sending Cripps to India. The British war cabinet was a coalition. The Labour Party, despite its performance when in office, still officially advocated freedom for India. The Labour ministers in the cabinet were, therefore, unwilling to be involved in the suppression of Congress. They also had grounds for believing that Congress would accept a reasonable offer. Churchill was also under considerable pressure from President Roosevelt. In the interests of both cabinet solidarity and the American alliance, a gesture of good will was necessary.

The 'Draft Declaration' Cripps took with him to India repeated the terms of the August offer of 1940, but went further on a number of points. India was conceded the right to leave the British Commonwealth if it wished. This implied that dominion status now meant the same as independence. Immediately after the war an elected Constituent Assembly would decide on a constitution without interference from the British, who would accept any agreed constitution with only one proviso: that any province had the right to remain outside the Dominion. There were various other clauses concerning such things as a treaty to guarantee 'British obligations'. As for immediate changes, there could be no fundamental ones for the duration of the war. But an interim system of government could be established, and the 'leaders of the principal sections of the Indian people' would be invited to join.

The choice of Cripps as negotiator was astute. He was an upper-class socialist and a friend of that other upper-class socialist, Jawaharlal Nehru. He had spoken often and with apparent sincerity on the right of Indians to choose their own form of government. Cripps also had an almost Indian puritanism which, coupled with the fact that he was a vegetarian, endeared him to Gandhi. Cripps believed that he could achieve a solution to the Indian problem, but he went hampered both by his brief, which offered pledges only redeemable after the end of the war, and by the taint of association, for he was a member of a cabinet headed by that consistent enemy of India's freedom, Winston Churchill.

Cripps began his talks in New Delhi on 25 March 1942. He met representatives from practically every facet of Indian political life, but there was one party not present at the discussions which was always in the minds of those who were—the Japanese army. While Cripps was talking, Japanese aircraft were bombing Indian cities. Though innumerable avenues were explored, there was no real desire for agreement. The Muslim league welcomed the implied recognition of Pakistan in the right for provinces to remain outside the new Dominion, but the statement was too vague for Jinnah. The same clause offended not only Congress but the communal Hindu Mahasabha and the Sikhs of the Punjab, who feared that the Muslim majority there would vote for non-accession. The Untouchables saw no guarantee that they would be protected from caste Hindus. Congress also resented the fact that the princes would be allowed representation in the Constituent Assembly. It also turned out that Cripps had exceeded his authority in suggesting that some form of 'national government' would be conceded, when all that the British government in London envisaged was an enlargement of the viceroy's executive council.

All these, however, were only the formal reasons for the rejection of the offer. Indian nationalists were unwilling to accept promises redeemable only in the distant and rather gloomy future. Faced with the possibility of a successful Japanese invasion there seemed no point in negotiating with the British. The view of the majority was expressed by Gandhi when he was reported, perhaps apocryphally, to have asked: 'Why accept a post-dated cheque on a bank that is obviously failing?' Far better to save energy for negotiations with the Japanese.

Talks did continue but the counter-proposals and arguments put forward were essentially a bluff. The overwhelming majority of Congress—and it was upon Congress that the success or failure of the Cripps mission depended—was quite prepared to gain India's freedom with the help of the first Asian power to strike a blow against Western imperialism. Japan's actions in China were unpleasant but this only worried a few sophisticated leaders such as Nehru. The rest responded favourably to the Japanese slogan 'Asia for the Asiatics' and put pressure upon their leaders. Under the circumstances there was no possibility whatsoever that the leaders would be allowed to accept less from the British than the majority thought it stood to gain from the Japanese.

Some attempt was made to keep the talks going. President Roosevelt's personal representative, Colonel Johnson, had conversations with Nehru and others. But his interference was resented by both the British and the Indian governments. Congress put forward the demand that the armed forces should be placed under the authority of an Indian member of the executive council, a proposal that was sure to provoke the unyielding opposition of the government of India. On receiving the proposal, the viceroy telegraphed his disapproval to London without informing Cripps. On 7 April a secret telegram reached Cripps from London, and from that moment his manner changed. So too did that of Congress. After a telephone call from the Mahatma, the Working Committee officially rejected the proposals. On 12 April Cripps departed for London, leaving only confusion and bitterness behind him.

The Congress leadership met again at the end of April and passed a resolution virtually dictated by Gandhi calling for resistance to the Japanese, but only in the form of non-violent non-cooperation. 'We may not bend the knee to the aggressor nor obey any of his orders. We may not look to him for favours nor fall to his bribes.' The government's defence effort was to be neither helped nor hindered. Congress would operate its own scorched-earth policy. Many of the Congress leaders were preparing to welcome the Japanese. A police raid on Congress offices in Allahabad discovered notes by Gandhi himself for a draft resolution assuring the Japanese 'that India bore no enmity' to them and that 'if India were free, her first step would be to negotiate with Japan'. The authenticity of these documents has been disputed but there is no reason to doubt the sentiments they express.

A few weeks later the Mahatma took action. He issued a provocative challenge to the British. Some dramatic gesture was called for. There was an atmosphere of tension and a growing desire among some Indians to seize their own freedom through revolutionary struggle. For the Mahatma, the thought that Bose might return in the baggage of the Japanese army was too much to contemplate. Gandhi's challenge was simple: let the British get out and 'leave India in God's hands'. Have no fears about the communal problem; the British created it and it would disappear once they had left. Anarchy, even internecine warfare, might follow 'for a time' but from it 'a true India will arise in place of the false one we see.'

The slogan Gandhi offered was 'Quit India.' With it, once again, the Mahatma touched a nerve and throughout India thousands rallied to the call. But what if the British did not respond (and it was highly improbable that they would)? Congress would have to follow up with a civil-disobedience campaign, and that could only help the Japanese. At Gandhi's retreat at Wardha, Nehru and the Mahatma argued over the decision and Nehru gained some concessions. Allied forces, Gandhi allowed, would be permitted to remain in India 'for the sole purpose of repelling a Japanese attack and helping China'. He was even willing to send 'India's ambassadors' to the Axis powers, not to beg for peace, but to show them 'the futility of war'. But Gandhi was immovable on the consequences which must follow the rejection of the call to 'Quit India.'

Nehru tried to persuade the Mahatma not to take his decision to the Working Committee. When the committee met early in July with no response from the British, Gandhi was adamant. He did not even seem to care about the possibility that non-violence would, as it always had done before, degenerate into violence. 'If in spite of precautions,' he said, 'rioting does take place, it cannot be helped.' There was opposition, but Gandhian blackmail worked once more. He would leave Congress and form another organization if his resolution was rejected. Naturally, it was not.

The AICC endorsed the resolution and presented an ultimatum to the British. If it was rejected and if Gandhi approved, the committee would sanction the 'starting of a mass struggle on non-violent lines on the widest possible scale'. The decision was with Gandhi, and he was quite sure what it would be. He had welcomed the committee's action.

The voice within me tells me I shall have to fight against the whole world and stand alone! . . . Even if the whole of India tries to persuade me that I am wrong, even then I will go ahead not for India's sake alone but for the sake of the whole world . . . I cannot wait any longer for Indian freedom. I cannot wait until Mr Jinnah is converted . . . If I wait any longer, God will punish me. This is the last struggle of my life.

As the meeting came to an end, Gandhi gave his blessing: 'Here is a mantra [a magical formula], a short one, that I give you. You may imprint it in your hearts and let every breath of yours give expression to it. The mantra is: "Do or Die". We shall either free India or die in the attempt.' His meaning was quite unequivocal—'This is a rebellion'—but his strategy was not very clear. Of course, this was typical of his political style.

There were no plans and it is possible that he had no intention of starting a campaign immediately. But it seems highly likely that he was once again in the grip of his inner voices. The quiet fury with which Gandhi spoke was obvious to all and not least the police agents who were present. Gandhi may have believed that his words would provoke the government, for he made no real distinction between non-violence and violence. In his exaltation, which one of the people present described as 'terrifying', he seemed to be hoping he might be killed and that his death would bring a national uprising.

Whatever Gandhi hoped for, the government could hardly stand idly by in the face of what was undoubtedly a call not to a few *satyagrahis* as before, but to the Indian people to rise in rebellion. The day after the speech, 9 August 1942, in one swift move the whole of the Working Committee and a number of other Congress leaders were arrested. Gandhi was taken to a palace belonging to the Aga Khan near Poona.

The arrest of the Congress leaders sparked an immediate response from the rank and file. There had been no concerted plan of action and all the demonstrations were spontaneous. In the cities, life was paralysed by close-downs and strikes. Vast crowds marched through the streets singing nationalist songs and demanding the release of the leaders. At first the demonstrations were peaceful but there were elements, extreme communalists, criminals and professional revolutionaries, who saw in the mass outburst of popular anger the chance they had been waiting for. The government too was edgy and so were the police. Crowds were fired upon and many were injured.

Facing what it believed to be a full-scale rebellion, the government imposed curfews and banned assemblies of more than five people. Congress was declared an illegal organization and its assets and records were seized. Mass arrests followed and many second-rank Congress leaders went underground. With the destruction of the Congress organization and the arrest of its executive leadership, new men took over the direction of the campaign. Some of these were of Gandhian leanings and tried desperately to keep the campaign non-violent. But in the climate of suppression and with the activities of communalists and criminals, who did not hesitate to stir up religious emotions so that they could loot and rape, there was no chance for moderation.

The frustrations of the young men were now released and they set about building up an organization that would parallel not only that of the British but also that of Congress. Where before they had been overshadowed by Gandhi, they now seemed to represent a real alternative leadership with a chance of capturing the masses while the others were in jail.

A wave of sabotage and criminally inspired violence spread across the country. By the middle of September, 250 railway stations had been destroyed or seriously damaged and 500 post offices attacked. A large section of the railway system was put out of action and communications so disrupted that the army on India's north-eastern frontier was deprived of its main channel of supply. Police stations and government buildings were set on fire and Indian members of the civil administration were threatened with death if they did not join the rebels. A number of those who refused were assassinated. The government used all the forces at its disposal. British troops were called in and aircraft were used against mobs, machine-gunning and bombing on at least five occasions. In some parts of the country the authorities even revived the terrible spectacle of public hanging.

Though the rebellion was undoubtedly serious, there was no mass uprising. Too many elements in the country kept aloof. The peasantry stayed in their fields, businessmen and the professional middle class continued to support the government. There was no sign of disaffection in the armed forces. The first phase of large-scale sabotage and violence was under control by the end of August. The second phase of isolated but still serious outbreaks was virtually over by the end of the year.

The failure of Congress to overthrow the British was welcomed by Conservatives in Britain. It only confirmed what they had been saying all along: Congress did not represent the mass of the Indian people. In the House of Commons in September, Winston Churchill claimed that the rebellion had at least made one thing clear: the 'non-representative character' of Congress and its 'powerlessness to throw into confusion the normal peace of India'. Considering the amount of damage that had been caused and that in certain parts of the country British rule had ceased and when he spoke had not been reimposed, Churchill's remarks were somewhat less than the truth.

Gandhi, however, had committed a grave error. Apart from the terror and suffering the 'Quit India' resolution had brought to so many while its sponsors sat comfortably in jail, it had left a vacuum in political India which was to be filled by divisive forces. When the time came for Britain actually to quit India, there were no longer just two parties—the British and the Congress—who had to agree upon the terms.

In May 1944, Gandhi was released from jail on grounds of ill health, although the government was still not prepared to release the other Congress leaders. Gandhi, the government insisted, had been let out only because his health was in danger. This was merely the excuse for releasing him, and the real reason was rather different. Despite Gandhi's apparent conversion to violence in 1942, the government was convinced that he had returned to his old ideas and could therefore once again be used as a mediator. It was, however, necessary to keep him away from the influence of more inflammatory Congress leaders such as Jawaharlal Nehru. If Gandhi could arrive at some arrangement with the Muslim League, it might still be possible to hand over power to a united India. One of Gandhi's first acts after his release was to visit Jinnah. The Mahatma's stay in prison had perhaps brought a belated sense of reality, for he offered Jinnah a formula which envisaged the possibility of partition; but there must, he insisted, be a provisional government at the centre for a transitional period. In spite of this offer, there was no possiblity of compromise with Jinnah. He could play too well upon Muslim fears that once there was a central government, it would be dominated by Congress, who would make it their business to see that the provinces could not secede. Jinnah smelt the coming of freedom and was not prepared to give way on anything. Unlike many Congress leaders, Jinnah did believe that the British really meant to leave India. They had by implication conceded the principle of Pakistan. Why then should he compromise when all he had to do was wait?

Gandhi had failed, and the government was not prepared to co-operate any further. It did not even bother to rearrest him. Labour members of parliament in London, sublimely ignorant of the nature of India's real problems, still called for the one thing that was impossible—the formation of a national government in Delhi. All this did was convince Jinnah that he was right in refusing to compromise. Most Labour members thought that Indian nationalists distrusted Britain and that if this distrust could be removed, all other problems would fade away. But the really dangerous distrust was between Indian and Indian, Congress and League, Hindu and Muslim, and to resolve it was beyond the power of Westminster. When it seemed that the end of the war and a British victory were in sight, all parties in India began to prepare for the final struggle. The Japanese no longer appeared as the probable liberators of India. Subhas Bose no longer threatened the old-guard leadership of Congress. The question now was whether the promises of the Cripps mission were genuine or not.

On 14 June 1945, the viceroy, Lord Wavell, who had succeeded Linlithgow in 1943, returned from a visit to London. The British government no longer included Labour ministers. The war in Europe had been over since May, and a general election was soon to take place. The proposals which Wavell took back to India in an attempt to break the old political deadlock had, however, been framed by the wartime coalition cabinet. The principal advance over the Cripps offer of 1942 was that the viceroy's executive council should be entirely Indian except for the viceroy himself and the commander-in-chief. The council would give equal representation to Muslims and Hindus. Wavell also announced that a conference would be called at Simla to discuss the proposals and that Congress leaders would be released from jail and invited to attend.

The Simla conference did take place, but it was what happened outside that was decisive. Congress assumed that the division of seats in the executive council between Muslims and caste Hindus was to be on a religious rather than a political basis. Congress maintained that it (Congress) was a *secular* body and would of course nominate Muslim members for the Muslim seats. Jinnah, however, was not prepared to accept this interpretation. The Muslim League, he claimed, was the sole representative of Muslim interests; consequently, the Muslim seats in the council should be filled by members chosen by the Muslim League. To this the viceroy could not agree, since the division of seats *was* intended to be purely religious. Jinnah refused to continue the negotiations and the first Simla conference broke up in failure.

Not that this mattered very much, Congress thought, for by now a new government had taken office in Britain. Churchill and the Conservatives had been rejected by the British electorate and the Labour Party had been swept to power with a large majority of the seats in parliament. Would Labour fulfil its often reiterated pledge to give India her freedom? On 15 August, as the war with Japan ended, the speech from the throne at the opening of parliament in Westminster contained these words: 'In accordance with the promises already made to my Indian peoples, my Government will do their utmost to promote in conjunction with the leaders of Indian opinion, the early realization of full self-government in India.'

With the Labour Party now in power in Britain, hope grew in India that self-government might really be only just around the corner. But that hope was conditioned by past experience. It seemed likely that the Labour government meant what it said, but this was not absolutely assured. The Labour government must be made to see that it was essential to grant India her freedom, not only in fulfilment of Labour promises but also in the interests of the British people. From the Congress point of view, this called for a new approach. On the one hand, the Labour government must be persuaded of the political sophistication of those to whom it would be handing power, and on the other it must be made quite clear that the alternative to freedom was violence.

This new approach meant that Gandhi had to be relegated to the background, for he was hardly a symbol of political maturity. While freedom had seemed far away, he was necessary both to Congress and the British. Now it was Nehru the socialist, charming and flexible, who was to fill the picture. Labour ministers would respond positively to his civilized, Western point of view; they could treat him as an equal. Gandhi, like some Indian Rousseau, was of another century, another and incomprehensible dimension, a man who spoke in the language of the pre-industrial world. As socialism had been spawned by industrial capitalism, it could hardly listen with patience and understanding to the spokesman of a back-to-nature philosophy. This was, in effect, the end of Gandhi as a moulder of major events. The mediator was no longer needed, the saint with his phalanx of illiterate peasants could be put aside. It was now the time for civilized negotiation between men who spoke the same unapocalyptic language. The stake was not freedom itself—for this seemed to have been agreed —but the pattern of that freedom. It was now Jawaharlal Nehru who spoke for Congress.

Gandhi's role in the terrible and bloody drama of the last days of British India was politically unimportant. As the leaders of Congress and the Muslim League fought their wars of succession, the Mahatma, rather like a constitutional monarch, impressive but powerless, hovered about the scene. Protocol was usually followed, the appearances of consultation observed, the necessary gestures of deference made, if possible, but Gandhi no longer represented Congress, and it is very doubtful whether he could have reimposed his influence *even if he had wanted to*. At this stage, when India's freedom was in sight, Gandhi was no longer interested in it. He had returned to the role of Hindu reformer which he had, in fact, never discarded. Now he was concerned, as he always had been, only with reducing violence. He was slowly coming to the conclusion that the division of India might be the only way to do this, and he was later to throw such influence as he still possessed on the side of those who were prepared to accept Pakistan. Gandhi did have a strong sense of reality—although it was not always apparent—but he interpreted every event in terms of its effect on his own self-imposed mission of reform; even the partition of India was not now to be allowed to stand in his way. Unlike the other Congress leaders, Gandhi had never yearned for political power, only that those in power should be favourable to his ideas of reform. Now, in 1947, he was seventy-seven years of age, and even saints do not live forever. Before he died, he wanted to put an end to the sufferings of the innocent. For him, the petty wrangling and intrigues at Delhi were of little importance in face of the greater menace which stalked India. And who, after a little thought, would deny that he was right?

The Mahatma, however, did not disclose the bias of his thinking. Inwardly, he remained committed to the granting of independence to an undivided India. But just as the rest of Congress was beginning to accept the fact that they were unlikely to get it and were becoming reconciled to the fact that a divided India was enough of the promised land from which they could make a profit, the Mahatma declared that he did not accept the principle of division, and began to preach the gospel

[249]

of unity—without, however, much of his old conviction. This was partly because he was becoming conscious of his inability to influence Congress as he had done in the past. Gandhi had sought to use Congress for his own narrow purpose, but Congress had used him in the struggle against the British. Now, when the prizes of freedom were within grasp, he was no longer needed at the helm. Saints are out of place when there is hard bargaining to be done between businessmen.

As late as 31 May 1947, Gandhi was still publicly against partition. 'Even if the whole of India burns,' he said at his prayer-meeting on that day, 'we shall not concede Pakistan, even if the Muslims demand it at the point of the sword.' Why did Gandhi utter such inflammatory sentiments at such a late date? There is no simple, clear-cut answer. Was he now hoping in some way to discredit those Congress leaders who had rejected him in their hour of triumph? Or was he attempting to dissociate himself in advance from any responsibility for Congress's decision to accept partition, a decision which would certainly come as a shock when it was made public? Gandhi had a very astute and agile mind, although he disguised it as much as possible behind contradictions of thought and action. It seems probable that, at this time, he had come to recognize that the Indian National Congress might no longer be the ideal instrument for his plans, and that he was slowly moving towards the possibility of some new political alignment. There is no doubt that he had had a number of discussions with orthodox Hindu politicians, one of whom—after Gandhi had been assassinated—told the author that the Mahatma had said that though he was against partition in principle, it might well be the only way of lessening communal tensions to such a level as would permit him to get on with his work of reform, but that nevertheless he would still fight it as hard as he could.

After independence, the orthodox Hindu political parties were to attack Gandhi violently for having played a double game, and it was such attacks which led finally, though indirectly, to his assassination by a Hindu extremist. It now seems sure that Gandhi *was* playing some sort of double game, but it has proved impossible to find out with any certainty just what the game was. Such 'evidence' as has emerged since the event has come from untrustworthy sources. But it does seem that, if Congress had moved away from Gandhi, Gandhi was also moving away from Congress as the pettiness of its leaders' ambitions came to light, and they fought over India for what they could get out of it.

On 15 August 1947, India celebrated its independence. Pakistan had already done so the day before. The Mahatma was not present at the celebrations in Delhi. He was in Bengal, trying his best to reduce the violence to which he now realized he had contributed as much as anyone. His actions, which included 'fasts to the death', had miraculous short-term effect, but in the end they were merely the most transient of dams against the flood of communal madness. The period from the day of independence to his assassination was for Gandhi one of anguish. He recognized the complete and utter failure of his ambitions. The new government of independent India was, he saw, not all that much different from the old government of imperial India: a *modern* government, apparently set upon pursuing policies that were repulsive to him.

In the intensity of his despair, it would not have been surprising that he welcomed death, and his murderer, as a friend. And there is some evidence in support of this. Ten days before the assassination, Gandhi's prayer-meeting was disturbed by the explosion of a small bomb. No one was hurt and pleas from the highest level, from Nehru and Patel, were made to the Mahatma, that he should accept police protection. He refused, as if it no longer mattered: 'God is my protector. If he cannot protect me, nobody can.' Of even more interest than the Mahatma's weary resignation is the fact that no attempt was made by the government to infiltrate plain-clothes policemen into the mansion of the cotton magnate, G. D. Birla.

The death of Gandhi could not have been more timely if it had been arranged by the government. In one sense, it was, for if it was not a constructive murder, it was a permissive one, encouraged by the laxity of the security services and of the police. Gandhi was already giving the appearance of opposition to those interests who now believed they had the formulae to open the Aladdin's cave of political patronage and power. Congressmen were taking bribes from businessmen to get them licences and lucrative contracts; they were profiting from black-market activities and putting pressure upon top civil servants to arrange appointments and promotions for their friends. Sickened by this display of greed, Gandhi had made the startling suggestion tht Congress should dissolve itself and form a Lok Seva Sangh, a Servants of the People Society. Over this and other matters, even Patel is reported to have said: 'The old man has gone senile.' For others, such 'senility' posed a potential threat.

There is no doubt that after the bomb explosion of 20 January, the elements of a conspiracy to murder the Mahatma were known to exist by the special branch of the police in Bombay, where the plot was hatched. An inquiry held twenty years later revealed that essential police documents were missing from the relevant files, and the inescapable conclusion from the evidence at that time is that nothing was done to warn Patel or Nehru, whose assassination was probably also planned, because there were important people who did not want anything done. The leader had become the victim.

POISONED HALO,
BATTERED CROWN

The relationship between the life of M. K. Gandhi and that of the British Indian Empire of his time was one of symbiosis—a mutually beneficial partnership between differing organisms. The relationships between the Myth of the Mahatma and the Myth of the Raj is parasitic—one feeding exclusively upon the other and inhibiting anything but the most superficial appreciation of the fundamental nature of either of them. In fact, it is essential that the mistletoe should appear to be not only purer than the oak but, somehow, greater than it.

But how? First, there must be a mixing of metaphors. The Mahatma will have to be cast as David against the Goliath of the Raj, Jack opposite the Giant. And, of course, he must be its killer. But was he? The answer, freed from myth, is, simply, no.

The answer can be simple, but the explanation must not be simplistic. That somehow the Mahatma—by illegally making salt, by persuading his followers to lie down in front of tramcars and daring the drivers to drive over them, by persuading them to offer their bodies in simple non-violence to be crushed and battered by the staves of the imperialist police, by a blackmailing appeal to the tyrant's better nature and fundamental morality—that somehow these simple stones in the slings of virtuous nationalists killed off the Raj, is simply not true. Yet it is the foundation upon which the myth of the Mahatma rests.

The Raj was brought to an end by an alliance of forces the Mahatma neither understood, nor wanted to understand. The structure of Empire, however impressive, however grandiose, always rests upon sand, and can be shaken by forces exterior to it. In the case of the Raj, this force was Japan. The first time the Japanese shook the Raj, hardly anyone noticed, least of all the British. In May 1905, the Japanese destroyed the Imperial Russian fleet at the battle of Tsushima. It was the first blow, and a successful one at that, by an Asian people against the white man. The second was to come nearly forty years later, when the Western empires in East and South-east Asia crumbled before the assault of Japanese armies. The Japanese encouraged nationalist movements in the territories they conquered, but they kept them under tight rein. However, the nationalists had established themselves, so that after the Allied victory in 1945, there was no going back to the old ways. This time the foundations of Empire had not just been shaken. The structure had been revealed as the lath and plaster of a stage-set, a *trompe-l'oeil* that no longer deceived.

There was another force, more powerful because more immediately recognized by the imperial power. More powerful, too, because it was not exterior to the imperial structure but an integral part of it. That force was the British people.

In the twentieth century, the masses have come to influence events in a very special way, for which there is little or no historical precedent. Generally speaking, in the past, authority maintained a studied indifference to the interests of the people as long as they remained quiet. One of the first concerns of the successful revolutionary who had made use of the people and their grievances to precipitate change, was to neutralize the violence he himself incited, to cut the people out of the calculations of politics, while leaving them in its vocabulary. But, as the twentieth century dawned, the place where the desires of the masses in the West could be expressed moved from the barricades to the halls of parliament. The masses became, in effect, respectable, part of the system of government, and authority could no longer rely upon their indifference. In Britain, the strengthening voice of the working classes demanded a better standard of living at home, even at the

[254]

expense of disposing of an empire abroad, and, in 1947, a 'people's government' in Britain finally had to make a choice —between hanging on to India or getting out. The choice it made was the choice of the British people, not, however, made consciously; there was no mass expression of popular opinion about India's freedom, for the majority of the British people were indifferent to the issue. But there were other issues about which they had positive, even passionate hopes, and any attempt to retain India might have prejudiced their fulfilment. The government, in effect, had no choice. Even a Conservative government would ultimately have realized it. The British people ceased to be interested in the British Empire, in its glories, responsibilities, virtues or vices, because they were concerned with their own welfare above all others, and were at last in a position to demand that their wishes be given priority.

Britain had emerged from World War II seriously weakened and needing all her resources for her own recovery. The Labour prime minister, Clement Attlee, was, above all, conscious that as the first Labour leader with a working majority in parliament, in fact an overwhelming majority, his primary responsibility was to those who had elected him to office. Labour voters were demanding a new deal and the redemption of long-stated promises. It seemed possible that Britain could be remade into a socialist paradise, and all pressures for doctrinaire reform were upon the prime minister. The Labour Party was prepared—had, in fact, been conditioned over the years—to sacrifice India as a prelude to the creation of a new Britain.

There was also the distinct probability that the electorate would not have tolerated any attempt by their government to use their sons, conscripted to fight against the Japanese in Asia, to maintain British rule in India by force. It is also probable that those civilians in uniform, having defeated the Japanese, and anxious only for repatriation and return to civilian life, would have refused to take part in repressive action in India. Some, indeed, had already mutinied over delays in repatriation. The Labour Party came into power ready for sacrifice just when it appeared to sensible men that there was no alternative but sacrifice. Ideology found an ally in the pragmatic. Out of weakness came forth statesmanship. The feeble grip transformed into the parting handshake could be made to appear as the final working out of a grand design which, in a sense, it was.

In one sphere the British people may have suffered from the dissolution of the Empire which began with India in 1947. Many felt a sense of personal loss as all the pomp of yesterday became one with Nineveh and Tyre. Empires are not merely political and economic realities: their possession becomes part of the national psychology of the imperial power. There is an 'identification' with empires that is not restricted to those of the upper and middle classes who benefited from them. Even those who bitterly attack the imperial adventure as a symbol of outmoded privilege still seem to feel a sense of constriction as the Union Jack flies over fewer and fewer of the detritus of Empire. Because this feeling is irrational, it has received irrational expression in such neo-imperial responses as the Suez affair of 1956, and the Falklands War of 1982. It is also an essential element in the commercialized nostalgia of TV series and epic movies, of the hyperbole of the tourist advertisement, in which the glories of the Raj can somehow be recaptured, at a price, by luxuriously railroading across India in a train made up of cars, once the private toys of maharajas and British governors.

What then of that other major component of the Myth of the Mahatma—the simplistic but immensely appealing image of the conflict between Good and Evil, between Darkness and Light, between the Mahatma and the 'satanic' government of the Raj? The question is simple, though the answer is not. How evil was British rule in India? The answer rather depends upon the yardstick, on any number of yardsticks of variable length. Putting aside theological criteria, the most reliable, though hardly infallible, unit of measure could be that of care and concern for the *majority*. It is one that can be applied to the behaviour of dominant minorities of any class, creed, colour, or time. If the yardstick used is a contemporary one, that is, of the time the British attempted to change the fabric of Hindu society, an ugly and repressive society, that attempt must be seen, though a failure, as progressive, worthy and humane. If the yardstick is of our own times, that of the Mahatma and his successors, then the judgement must just as surely stand, for Hindu society remains ugly and repressive nearly forty years after the departure of the British.

The British who first conquered and then ruled India were often better and certainly no worse than their contemporaries of other nations. The popular image of idiots wearing monocles and playing polo, occasionally vicious Bertie Woosters, is a caricature of the Marxist music hall. 'Silly asses' neither conquer nor rule empires. There were no saints in British India and surprisingly few sinners—considering the opportunities available. The only valid criticism that may perhaps be made of the guardians of the Empire in its last years is that they were intellectually dull. But the Raj was a bourgeois empire and had the virtues as well as the vices of that often justifiably maligned class. It may well seem plumbing bathos to describe the greatest empire the world has ever known, and, one hopes, ever will know, as well-meaning, on the whole humane, and eventually dull! But the comparison is not with some ideal empire, if there could be such a thing, but with those actual ones of other European powers, and, indeed, with the United States in the early years of its conquest of the Philippines. It is hard to envisage the Dutch or the French, or those who were among the first to use the dumdum or expanding bullet on their colonial subjects, tolerating a Gandhi, let alone having the wisdom to collaborate with one. The Raj was a mixture of the good, mediocre, and a little bad, not a series of Amritsars or a sort of continuing Vietnam.

If the Darkness of the Evil was perhaps a middling grey, how Light was the Good?

Gandhi claimed: 'My life is my message': not what he *said* but what he *did*. Gandhi's life was an Indian life, and the message is Indian too. By the time Gandhi returned to India for the last time, in 1915, the traces of his foreign experience were already fading, leaving behind only the universalist rhetoric designed to appeal to foreigners. His sense of political reality, of the desirable and the possible which is the essence of that reality, was a product of his Indian experience, fundamentally of the British who ruled India. Gandhi frequently claimed to discern in the British a core of morality and goodness. And he was right. There was always a limit beyond which the British were not prepared to go in India. That limit, despite Amritsar, was always far short of total ruthlessness.

It was this experience of a 'gentle' imperialism that must have led to the fatuosity, naïveté and callousness of the Mahatma's advice to the Jews in Germany in 1938, that they should offer mass civil disobedience to the Nazis. In 1938, Gandhi was not alone in his unwillingness to accept the true horror of the 'Final Solution'. But even after the dimensions of that horror were revealed, he continued to insist that if the Jews had followed his advice, they would have won a moral victory, even though they would have died just the same. Gandhi could not imagine a government unamenable to his variety of blackmail.

The definition 'Indian', though adequate to describe Gandhi's political awareness, is not enough to define other and more important areas of his life and influence. The definition must be narrowed: Gandhi's life was a Hindu life, and his message was Hindu also. Hindu morality is centred upon the self and self-realization. It has little concern for others. One need look no further than the cruelty of Gandhi's relations with those nearest to him: the harsh treatment of his children, who could not live up to his inhuman rectitude, his callous destruc-

[258]

tion of marriages and families, which stemmed from his deeply Hindu hatred of women, those terrible distractions along the way of *brahmacharya*. Gandhi's pursuit of *brahmacharya*, whatever the cost to others, moves from the tragic to the risible with his continuing experiments with sex. In his seventies, he was still sharing his bed with young girls, still trying to conquer and control his sexuality, still worrying about a wet-dream he had in 1936, but caring nothing for the psychic damage he might be causing by his experiments. Gandhi was a maimed personality. As George Orwell suggested in his 1949 essay, the Mahatma lacked love, ordinary human love.

The damage Gandhi inflicted during his search for *brahmacharya* was upon comparatively few, and they, in the main, were volunteers. But the damage inflicted by his idealization of poverty and of the poor was upon millions, damage almost incalculable and apparently endless. His own ostentatious poverty was sustained by an elaborate, and expensive, infrastructure. As one of his followers, the Indian poet Sarojini Naidu, put it: 'It costs a great deal of money to keep Gandhiji living in poverty.' But living like a poor man is very different from being one. The Mahatma's 'simple' life sanctified poverty, gave it the appearance of the holy, allowed it, in fact, to remain where it had always been, on the lowest levels of the Hindu order of society. The Untouchables, the poorest and the most socially coerced of India's people, were given a new name by the Mahatma: *Harijans*, children of God. It has made little difference to them, even though they were given a wide measure of protection and support in the constitution of independent India. Hindu society is not, as so many non-Hindus seem to think, a life-denying society, but it is a life-fixing one. The children of God are still the very least of his people, and any preferential treatment they may be entitled to is deeply resented by caste Hindus. Physical violence against Harijans is still commonplace, their poverty essentially unchanged.

Apart from uplifting statements and a fast or two, Gandhi did nothing to raise the status of the poorest. It is not surprising for one who had such a high opinion of the spiritual value of poverty. Gandhi was never a progressive reformer. He was essentially anti-modern. He did not look forward to a Golden Age, but back to one that had never existed; to a Hindu society somehow cleaned up and purified rather than remade. The dead weight of Hindu atavism, disguised in Gandhian shibboleths, lies heavy upon India today, encouraging the dark forces in the Hindu psyche, creating and sustaining illusion. In India it is still the illusion that usually has the last word. The imagined myth triumphs over the real. But it need not be so. Not even in India, and certainly not in the West. The Raj is dead. No one would seek to emulate it. The Mahatma is dead. That such a man should be considered an exemplar in the West is indicative of another sort of poverty inside Western culture itself.

BIBLIOGRAPHICAL NOTE

In writing *The Myth of the Mahatma* I have drawn upon three of my earlier books: *The Last Years of British India* London and Chicago 1963; *British India 1772–1947: A Survey of the Nature and Effects of Alien Rule* London and New York 1967; and *Nehru: A Political Biography* London 1971 New York 1972.

During his lifetime the Mahatma wrote millions of words, most of them of strictly ephemeral interest. However all of them are being republished in what is becoming an almost endless series of memorial volumes sponsored by the Indian government. Worth reading is Gandhi's own autobiography: *The Story of My Experiments with Truth*. Many editions are available.

Almost as many words have been written *about* Gandhi. Among the large number of biographies in English, Robert Payne: *The Life and Death of Mahatma Gandhi* London and New York 1969, can be recommended for its accuracy and lack of bias.

Two works by very different authors consider the mind of the Mahatma, and come to very different conclusions, Arthur Koestler: *The Lotus and the Robot* London and New York 1961, and Erik Erikson: *Gandhi's Truth* London 1976 New York 1977. Koestler sees Gandhi as a Hindu obscurantist, Erikson as a sort of saint.

Ved Mehta: *Mahatma Gandhi and his Apostles* New York 1977 London 1978, wittily penetrates to the core of the myth, while V. S. Naipaul: *India, a wounded civilisation* London and New York 1978, contains illuminating insights into Gandhi and the Hindu view of society which still dominates in independent India, in spite of the superficial modernity of its government.

INDEX